ANTHOLOGY OF POETRY
BY
YOUNG AMERICANS

1994 EDITION
VOLUME CXXXVI

Published by Anthology of Poetry, Inc.

©*Anthology of Poetry by Young Americans*®
1994 Edition
Volume CXXXVI
All Rights Reserved

Printed in the United States of America

To submit poems for consideration in the 1995
edition of the *Anthology of Poetry by Young
Americans*®, send to:
>   Anthology of Poetry
>   PO Box 698
>   Asheboro, NC 27204-0698

Authors responsible for originality of poems
submitted.

The Anthology of Poetry, Inc.
148 Sunset Avenue
Asheboro, NC   27203

ISBN: 1-883931-01-0

Anthology of Poetry by Young Americans® is a
registered trademark of Anthology of Poetry, Inc.

Five short years have past since the first edition of the <u>Anthology of Poetry by Young Americans</u> was published. These five years of editing the anthology have convinced us that children are natural poets. Poetry is play with language and language is still so new to them that it is a perfect fit. This poetry is filled with their ticklish energy and unrestrained concern. It is the best medium for young writers to express themselves. When they don't know the word for the thought or feeling they are trying to express they simply make one up. You won't find multiquizically in any dictionary but its meaning is clear. We try to present the poems as the author wrote them, in their format and punctuation. We of course corrected misspelled words, unless they added something to the poem, such as purrfect when describing a cat. We had a wonderful time editing the 1994 edition of the <u>Anthology of Poetry by Young Americans</u> and hope you enjoy reading the poetry as much as we did. We would like to extend a special thanks to all the poets who participated and are expecting great things from them in the future.

The Editors

REFLECTIONS

What I see
staring up at me,
a person
in the water,
a small
pale
delicate
familiar person.
I know her,
for it is only me
that I see.
Rain has started...
Where it once was
glassy pools
of my reflection,
is now ruffled mirrors of waves.
The girl has faded
and I trudge on
through the depthless
large puddle where
the girl once was.

Courtney Hornberger
Age: 11

THE STORM

A clap of thunder
And then it
Begins.
Swirling dragon clouds
Of deep purple and midnight
Coil onto the darkening sky.
The dragon
Awakes.
Breathing lightning fire,
It strikes its victims
And burns the land.
It is
Angry.
The only source of
Relief
Is the violent downpour
Of rain and the
Cold, unfriendly mist.
The dragon's breath,
Powerful and mighty,
Sweeps the earth.
Its smooth body
Is rippling with
Force and
Gleaming scales.
The dragon is unstoppable
Until...
The shining
Knight in armor comes
From around the hills
In the east.
Daylight.
The dragon retreats

As quickly as it
Came.
It is afraid.
Peace returns to the
Land.
The world returns to
Softly-singing
Calm.

Tiffany Lee
Age: 13

Waves of water crash,
And slashing through the night's darkness,
Bolts of lightning flash.

Dougland Chu
Age: 13

WINTER

Snow falls to the ground,
Little animals are sleeping
In their warm and nice caves
The white snowflakes fall to
The ground, and then all is
Quiet in the cold snow.

Melorose Lim
Age: 8

LIFE IS A PRECIOUS GIFT

Life is very precious to me
It is so nice to see.
Life is unfair sometimes though
But overall, it is colorful like a rainbow.
I know my life will never fall apart
If I always follow what's in my heart.
Life's full of great surprises and tests
God gives us signs we can see.
Therefore, I think it's best for all of us
To make our lives the best they can be.

Joaquin Ayala

THOUGHTS

Are you here?
Despair, loneliness
You are here.
Happiness, joy
Do you smile?
Sadness, anger
You do smile.
Glory, gladness
Are you simple?
Wonder, hope
I am simple.

Jenny Tam

RAIN

A rainy day to
me is the best
much much better
than all the rest
the feeling of the
water drops on
my skin is the
best sensation
that's ever been.

If it continues
to pour more
than four days
I say to myself
'Boy, how I hate the rain.'

Then after a
long hot summer's
day I say to myself,
'Boy, where's the rain?'

Ricky Collins
Age: 13

LOVE

Love is
a gift, a gift of joy to share.

Love is
endless, an endless message in life.

Love is
tears, joy, and pain.

Love is
a mystery, that conquers all.

Love
breaks hearts, and pulls them together.

Love is
hard to accomplish, yet it fades away easily.

Love is
something you should hold onto, and not let go.

Love is
the people around you,
your friends and especially your family.

Love is
something we have created,
forgot at times, and have remembered.

Through everything three things
Have kept us together
Love, faith, and hope
In each other.

Love is change.

Love takes chances.

Love is us!

Kalina R. Lawrence
Age: 13

GOING PLACE TO PLACE

I like going high
I like going west   I like going east
I like going low

I like to go to Hawaii and do the hula.
Then go to Mexico and grab an enchilada.
And fly to Scotland,
To play the bagpipes with a little tune.
Then go to Spain to shake hands with Columbus.
And then, jump to China and climb Mount Everest
Until I make it to the top.
Then go to Japan to see
If I have more strength to climb Mount Fuji.
Next, I shall go to the Philippines
And video camera the waterfalls
While I pick some wild flowers.
Oh! never mind! I'll just go to the library
And check out a book.

April Joy Damian
Age: 9

MY BROKEN WRIST

I broke my wrist oh what a shame!
It hurts so much, there's so much pain.
I fell on it and twisted it and then I knew
I must of broken it.
I missed a single day of school,
Oh I must of been a fool,
To jump up high to kick a ball,
Instead to miss it and then to fall.
Then right away, I learned a lesson,
'Be careful when you play and pay attention!'

John Restauro
Age: 13

FEELINGS

Feelings are special to you and me.
We just don't know what to do or see.
And when you come home,
You feel like just being alone.
Sometimes you cry and sometimes you pout.
But sometimes you feel like just shouting out.
It's hard to pass your feelings by
But then what you do is just want to cry.
Share them with your friends that's what you should do
And maybe they'll go away as simple as feelings do.

Monica Onopa
Age: 13

MY FEELINGS FOR YOU

This is a funny feeling.
I just can't stop fantasizing.
It's too hard to explain.
I know this is insane.
When you're near,
I start to fear.
I don't feel the same.
I talk lame.
My knees start to shake.
I try to act fake.
I know that I should ignore it,
Or maybe I'll try not to show it
This is crazy.
How could this be?
My heart is giving in.
Liking you is not a sin.
Sometimes I wish you'll feel it too.
But I know I can't make you to.
This is a gift from above,
Is this lust or is it love?

Alnette Dela Rosa
Age: 13

A ROSE

The sweetest flower that
blooms,
I give you as we part.
For you it may be just
a rose.
But for me it's my whole
heart.

Teresa Dominguez
Age: 12

LOVE IS..

Love is an emotion, for I cannot describe.
Some use it in the wrong way,
Others may use it to bribe.
Love is such a strong word
For no one has the same definition.
You shouldn't use love unless you mean it.
Love is like the world, how'd it come to be.
I guess it'll just be a question to me.

Only if I knew what love meant.
I'd probably say it at right times,
Not just say it if it comes to my mind.
Love is a powerful word,
For I don't know what it means.
I guess it'll just be a question unknown to me.

Morgan R. Sanders
Age: 13

HALLOWEEN

The night is young,
The nightingale has sung,
Spirits come in line,
Sending shivers up your spine,
Unhallowed ghosts appear,
Vanishing into air,
Screams heard upstairs,
Silence then appears,
Mutants in the street,
Monsters at your feet,
Trick or treat,
Give me something good to eat.

Joe Zhang
Age: 13

MY LOVE

Today I am here
tomorrow I might be gone
but if I die, I just haven't
had enough courage and
the time to tell you how I
feel or show you that my
love can be real
but my love will always
be here waiting for you
my love will always stay

Dexter Mendiola
Age: 13

HAVE YOU EVER HAD...A BEST FRIEND

Have you ever had someone special in your life,
Who you shared your secrets all through the night?
Have they ever been like a sibling to you,
During the good times, the bad times,
And those times in fright?

Have they ever helped you out,
When you needed a good listener to talk to?
Have you ever wondered about your friendship,
If that friend was the kind that could really be true?

Have you ever thought they would leave you,
As you argue and protest over who's wrong or right.
Have you ever had a friend like that,
Then don't ever let them leave or go out of your sight.

Have you ever had a best friend,
Do they stay by your side through a billion?
Have you ever had a best friend,
Who's one in a million?

Have I ever had a best friend,
Who was all of these things and many more too?
Have I ever had a best friend,
Of course, luckily for me
　　----------it's you!

Jessica de Leon
Age: 13

12

A WHISPER

What does a whisper feel like?
A funny kind of question to ask.
To me a whisper feels like a kiss
From a mother to her child.
As if a cloud were talking in your ear.
A whisper to me,
Can set you free,
Or make you close in even more.
To me there are all kinds of whispers,
Soft, loud, but not too loud
Because then it could turn into a yell.
Secret whispers, whispers that make you feel like
You'll burst if you hold them in any longer.
Whispers can be friendly or they can be mean.
If you tell a good whisper
A good whisper will come to you
But if you tell a bad whisper about someone,
Someone will tell a bad one about you.
So be careful when you tell a whisper,
Or even if you hear one,
Because a whisper can be as weak as an ant,
But then pop back up as strong
As the first thing you think about
When you're about to fall asleep.
And you know that feeling
Because every day,
Every person on the earth
Looks forward to every night.
To me, a whisper is like a dream.

Elana Altman
Age: 10

IT WAS MIDNIGHT

It was Halloween night,
The faces of the jack-o-lanterns were bright.
I started for home not knowing I was alone.
I walked into the night,
When a bright light came over the night.
Suddenly I was filled with fright.
A witch walked toward me,
'Come with me my dear', she said.
I pretended not to hear
Also tried to hold back the tears.
I remembered there was a ditch.
I threw her in,
And I hope I don't see any of her kin!

Sarah Adler-Milstein
Age: 10

ROSES IN THE WINTER

Red roses in the winter
So brightly colored
So delicate are their petals
Such a sweet smell in winter
When the rose dies it leaves a stem with no petals
The winter rose is lovely
So when it dies don't cry
Because it comes again to bloom
In the wintertime.

Veronica Moreno
Age: 14

BOOKS

I think that I will never look
And find anything as good as a book.

Books are neat,
Books are cool,
I learned to read them
At my school.

Books are fun,
Books are great,
I read them so much
I am sometimes late.

Books can take you many a place,
Under the earth or outer space.

So whenever you chance
To find a book,
Take a peek,
Take a look.

Herschel Pecker
Age: 9

TO THE FAMILY I CANNOT SEE

To the family I cannot see,
We're on different sides of the moon,
But on the same family tree.
Its branches stretch farther than the eye can see,
Yet no matter how high I am on the tree,
Or how far the branches carry me,
We still meet at the roots of the tree.

To my brothers across the sea,
I have forgotten you as you have forgotten me,
An inevitability of being separated by an endless sea.
Maybe a slave or maybe free
But we will meet at the roots of the tree.

To my brothers who have denied me,
Things may change and time may pass,
But that tree has kept growing fast.

It wrapped its branches,
Around those great and small,
Around men who stand and men who crawl,
Around enemies on different sides of the wall.
And though you pushed you lost the fight.
You tried to break free with all your might,
By denying your brothers their God given rights,
Pushing them down as you raised to great heights.
But my brothers you are a part of me
And, we are all stuck on this colossal tree.

So, unless we stop, realize, and see,
That we all meet at the roots of the tree,
Man will go on treating man inhumanely.

Kaylah Marin
Age: 16

SILENCE

Silence is alive
She screams and yells
And laughs and giggles
She follows a river
That twists and squiggles.
She jumps on a boat
That shall follow the sea,
Making sound seem like paradise
And silence, misery.

You will wake up at night
And listen to silence -
Her sound that takes over
And makes your ears hum,
But her sound can be broken
By one single sound,
Then she will take over
And...
Silence will rule.

Lindsay Ward
Age: 11

WINTER

It's clean, it's clean, it's legwarmers.
It's an ice-skating, fireplace lighting day.
It's hibernating, cocoa flavored sniffy,
With the children snowflakes scattered at their play.

It's the night like a cold blanket,
And the sidewalks overlaid,
With a glaze of lavender-white,
Like a frozen flower parade.

It's the cold wind blowing, blowing,
And the stars like startled glass,
While the cold wind keeps on blowing,
In a nutcracker dance.

Then the thin blue shivering evening,
Like an ice cube on the walk,
And the windows creaking open,
With a crisp amount of talk.

It's the way the trees are swaying,
And Jack Frost kisses them with flakes,
And the sky departing sweetly,
Like a little girl on skates.

It's clean! It's clean! It's winter!
My favorite time of year!

Hannah Lew
Age: 13

AMBITION

Ambition is a star.
Shining up in the sky.
A jewel that fulfills all greed,
But work is the ladder you climb.

When you don't work hard,
A cloud appears, blocking your way
So you can't continue until
You work hard again.

But when you reach
That distant star that
Belongs to you alone,
You'll look down at the
Ladder you climbed,
Higher and higher, rung by rung.
All the years of work paid off.

Then you look up to
Another star.
A new goal for you.
Still your own and
You climb the ladder again.

Wendra Liang
Age: 10

October is a time when Nature says it is going to snow
And animals gather food so they can live and grow.
Gold and red leaves fall on the ground,
Chipmunks run all around.
That's why October is the best month around.

Thomas McKinley
Age: 9

FEAR AND LONELINESS

Fear and loneliness are best friends.
First Loneliness comes,
And takes you over with its powerful grasp,
As if that's not enough,
Fear jumps in a few seconds later,
And it puts in your head,
All the things that could happen,
Like someone going down a list.
They both take over your thoughts, your body,
They're both especially powerful at night,
When the only lights in your room,
Are the street lights,
Seeping through the windows,
Making deep, dark shadows.
In the morning;
At the first sight of dawn,
They flee.

Kathryn Reilly Robertson
Age: 10

ODE TO THE MOON

Oh, Moon!
Why are you so bright in the sky?
Moon, you are just like a beautiful girl.
Does the goddess really live on you?
Who gave birth to you, Moon?
Was it the sun or the king of the sky?
Why don't you come out in the morning, Moon?

Mario Cheung
Age: 8

TOMORROW

Tomorrow is another day
  When we can start anew;
Our chance to correct today's mistakes,
  A list of problems we shall undo.

If yesterday we were mean
  Tomorrow we shall say
That we are sorry for the bad we did,
  Please do not be saddened or dismayed.

Tomorrow can be something
That we can picture in our mind;
With many things we can't predict,
Many surprises we may find.

Chrystal Fontanilla
Age: 12

ODE TO THE MOON

Oh, Moon!
You look like a big, round balloon.
You smell like perfume.
You taste like sweet candy.
You sound like fireworks.
You feel like a teddy bear.
Does the goddess really live on you?
Are you always round like a balloon or
Do you like looking like a banana?

Kim Mai Tsai
Age: 8

OUR WONDERFUL WORLD?

What ever happened
To our wonderful world?
Why do we need locks on our doors
When people long ago didn't
Because there was no crime?
Why are there people living in the street?
Why are people dying from diseases?
There are so many questions
About the world
Pollution and littering that
All I can ask is
WHY!

Meredith Moy
Age: 10

ODE TO THE MOON

Oh, Moon!
Round and bumpy like an orange.
You glisten at night with all your might.
And give everyone light at night.
But in the morning...
You are gone
And the sun comes out instead.
Oh, Moon,
Where do you go when the sun comes out?
Do you go to the circus to be rolled around?
I don't know...
Oh, Moon!

Joyce Yuan
Age: 8

ODE TO THE MOON

Oh, Moon!
You feel hot and sweaty,
You taste like candy.
You look like a watch.
Do you like to be a full moon?
Or not a full moon?
You smell like smoke,
Because you are very hot.

Daisy Van
Age: 8

COMPUTERS

I like computers.
Computers are cool.
We use them at home.
We use them at school.
We learn new things to make us smart.
Even computers can make good art!

Brooks Washington
Age: 9

LONELY

Sitting in the corner of a dark room
A small boy sheds a tears,
Waiting for someone to comfort him filled with fear,
The silent and lonely room gives him a scare,
As he clings to a pillow for something to bear.
Thinking of life and feeling hurt,
He wishes everything were different
Instead of being treated like dirt.
Watching the clock as the hours fly by
Asking the same question over and over again,
Why?
Why did it have to happen to me?
Doesn't anyone know how could this be?
It's hard for people to express how they feel,
But it's something you can't ignore it's real.

Christine V. Basto
Age: 13

ODE TO THE MOON

Oh, Moon!
You reminded me of an oatmeal cookie,
Or a big grapefruit.
You taste bitter like a kiwi on lime.
Your yellow light brightens the nighttime sky.
You feel smooth.
Why do you change your shape every now and then?
You look like a part of a smile so bright.
The stars around you glitter and sparkle.
I look out the window and there you are...
Hiding behind a tree!
You are like a night light in a dark room.

Crystal Lim
Age: 8

ODE TO THE MOON

Oh, Moon!
You look like a cookie.
Tasting as sweet as an apple.
Smelling like a mooncake eaten at night.
Feeling as cold as icy snow.
Does the Moon Lady really live on you?
Where do you go when the morning light comes?
Do you go into the sun?
You sound like a cat sleeping in the night.

Nancy Duong
Age: 8

FRIENDS

They try to listen to your concerns
And your personal troubles,
They try to comfort you in some way,
They try to share the same hobbies
You have assembled,
They try to always find something nice
To say everyday.

When you are lonely they are always there,
When you are sad they will always cheer me up,
When you are angry they always
Calm me down everywhere,
When you are happy they always gave me faces
Cute as a little pup.

Forever...they will always be my closest supporters,
Forever...they will be the kindest ones
I will grasp onto,
Forever...they will truly be the best understander,
Forever...they will always be as industrious
As the animals eating at the zoo.

Friends, they will always be on your side,
Friends, they always will be the best you can find.
Friends, they will always be as gentle
As the evening tide,
Friends, they always and always will be mine
...forever...

Felix Lau
Age: 13

HAVE A HAPPY THANKSGIVING

Roses are red violets are blue.
Have a happy Thanksgiving
From me to you.

Anne Marie Carr
Age: 8

ODE TO THE MOON

Oh, Moon!
Shining brightly at night.
Oh, Moon!
You are the most beautiful sight!

Oh, Moon!
You smell like rocks in space.
Oh, Moon!
Craters cover your face.

Oh, Moon!
I think you taste bitter and sweet at the
same time.
Or maybe sour,
like a lemon or lime.

Oh, Moon!
You are silent with a haunting sound,
haunting astronauts all around.

Nance Yuan
Age: 8

Roses are red,
Violets are blue.
Turkeys are good.
How about you?

Rosa W. Yee

MY LITTLE BROTHER

My little brother as you can see
Is quite different from you and me.
Yes, he eats, runs, and sleeps,
Calls for Mom with crying weeps.
Yet, my little brother as you can see
Is quite different from you and me
I ask him questions-when, where, and why!
He answers me with a bunkum reply.
'Where does the sun go at night?' I said.
'He goes to sleep in his soft bed.'
'What are clouds made of?' I inquired curiously.
He shouted, 'Gumdrops and cotton candy!'
I asked, 'Why do the stars twinkle so bright?'
He answered, 'They're glitter glued to the night.'
'What makes flowers smell so?'
'The brilliant colors that make them glow.'
My little brother as you can see
Is quite different from you and me.

Jo Ann Etorma
Age: 13

Roses are red,
Violets are blue.
Thanksgiving is a holiday, just for you.

Ricky Shum
Age: 8

THE KNOCKOUT

The crowd stood waiting
The fight had begun
The two men stood ready
This wasn't for fun.

The boxers went at it
And showed no mercy
The bout was between
'Iron Mike' Jones and 'No Mercy' Percy.

All of a sudden
The whole thing was over
The champ was planted in the ground
Like a four-leaf clover.

The fans couldn't believe it
They all stood in awe
The champ was knocked-out
With a hook to the jaw.

Eugene A. Moggia, Jr.
Age: 13

THANK YOU

Thank you for the sun above.
Thank you for the snow-white dove.
Thank you for dew drops
Upon the green grass.
Thank you for the rain
That falls upon the glass.
Thank you for all I eat.
Thank you for the snow and sleet!
Thank you!

Adelle Martin
Age: 9

ON THANKSGIVING DAY

On Thanksgiving Day
My family had turkey, pudding and pie.
But I stayed in my room.
For I was having my doom.
For there was a hundred turkeys, all in my room.
I called for help.
But nobody was there.
For they were all saying
A Thanksgiving Day prayer.
I called and I called but it was no use.
When I started crying the turkeys went downstairs.
But I wish they had not.
Because when I came down my family was gone.

Kathleen Nolan
Age: 8

Halloween is scary
Halloween is fun
I go trick or treating just for fun
I see lots of ghosts
I see lots of witches
I see lots of cats
But the most I see are bats

Jessica Li
Age: 8

SOMETIMES IT SEEMS LIKE SHE'S THE ONLY ONE LEFT

Sometimes itseems like she's the only one left,
The only person who would be me,
And yet another creature.
Sometimes it seems like she's
The only one left I can talk to,
Never does she tell my feelings to anyone.
Sometimes it seems like she's the only
One that is visible to my own eyes,
Sensitive, warm, gentle,
And beyond anyone's expectations.
Sometimes it seems like she's the only one
That I can hear talking softly in small whispers,
Not knowing what to expect.
Sometimes it seems like she's the only one
That I can talk to, see, feel, hear, and depend on,
And that is myself.

Gloria Pan
Age: 11

THE SKY

The sun is bright.
The sky is blue.
Little clouds are going through.
Birds soaring through the sky.
I just wish I could fly.

Wilbur Leong
Age: 8

THE OCEAN

The ocean waves call to you,
they want to tell you something.
They have a secret to share
with you, don't you want to know?
The ocean will take you with the
undertow, let it take you out.

Down below the boats,
there lay a great world.
Rocks, stars, wildlife
live there without fear.

Fish swim in schools,
they learn quite a lot.
But no one will ever know,
unless you go and explore,
the ocean world.

Elizabeth Tafolla
Age: 13

A WHISPER FEELS LIKE....

A whisper feels like a horse's nose,
Soft and gentle,
A whisper feels like a feather
 in your ear,
Tickling away,
A whisper feels like
 a few drops of rain,
Telling you something
 you might want to know,
Sometimes when you don't want
 to hear the news,
It sounds like a thunderstorm
 that you can't stop,
A whisper feels like a cozy fire,
When you are roasting marshmallows
 'til they're black,
A whisper feels like a meadow
 with tall grass,
Swaying against your leg,
With a soft breeze rolling by,
A whisper can also feel like a sour lemon
 when you hear it,
But, it can also feel like
 a bright red strawberry,
With great news.

Nancy Allen
Age: 10

FEAR...

Fear looks like a big, black horse,
Wildly galloping out of the night,
With an unseen rider,
  That is fear.

Fear sounds like,
Long nails, screeching across a blackboard,
Sizzling lizards in a big witch's cauldron,
Crows cackling in a big, dark forest,
Tigers growling, very near, too near,
  That is fear.

Fear smells like,
Smoke from a fire that burned a house down,
Like black tar, being poured on the street,
Like a thousand skunks,
A smell like rotting wood,
  That is fear.

Fear tastes like,
Popsicles that are too cold,
Hot soup that scalds your mouth,
Old cheese, and sour milk,
Like ice cubes, dancing in your mouth,
  That is fear.

Fear feels like,
A raven's wing, brushing your face,
A cold wave, going down your back,

Little cold fish, swimming in your stomach,
And up and down your spine,
    That is fear.

Deirdre Costello
Age: 10

SLEEPY

Sleepy.
Dreamy.
Morning?
Sink down into pillow.
Awake.
My eyes are open.

Anna Krasno
Age: 9

THANKSGIVING

Thanksgiving is a good day.
You eat cranberries and eat pumpkin pies.
You eat turkey.
You eat the stuffing.
When we do this it is on Thanksgiving.
You will pray for your family on that day.

Anthony B. Ipac
Age: 7

I'M COLORADO

You may know me,
By Dener, my capital,
Or my great Rockies,
That are ever so tall.
But what's wrong with you humans,
Don't you ever look up!

I really love rain,
Heck! Have it every day,
Oh yes, precipitation,
Rain, hail, snow any Ol' way.

I make clouds,
Do more than meet,
Make them perform lightning,
What a great feat!

Big bolts little blots,
All the same,
Few forks, many forks,
For which have no name.

Yes I'm more than sky,
For all you people with a sore neck,
Mountains that stand up high,
And rivers that flow like heck.

This brings us to the Garden of the Gods,
With its pentacles and deep crags,
People get paid from it,
With Indian jewelry, and fancy paper bags.

Yes, I'm Colorado,

The land,
Where clouds,
Do more than meet.

Adrian Andrejeff
Age: 12

When do pigs fly?
How do snails glide?
Do dogs eat pigs?
Do pigs eat snails?
I wonder if a dog could eat a pie!
Will he stuff turkey in its mouth?
Oops!
I forgot pigs fly with porcupines.

Jonathan Wilkinson

I DON'T WANT TO MOVE

Roses are red, violets are blue
I wish it was Thanksgiving again don't you?
I can't wait for the turkey or the pumpkin pie,
And all I can do is look at the sky.
I don't want to move, I don't want to budge,
I can only think of that pudding with fudge.

Alicia Gray
Age: 8

CATS

Cats are magnificent animals,
They jump with ease,
They walk without hesitation.

Ryan Salonga
Age: 13

MAPLE

A maple sat tranquil,
Whispering to the wind
That whistled through its branches,
As it bowed down
To shake hands
With the blades of grass
That grew around
Its gnarled roots.

Hannah Miller
Age: 13

FROGS

There are not enough frogs in the world.
They hop and jump freely
And croak out their tunes for all
The world to hear; sometimes
Croaking timid,
In fear.
Their little green bodies
Bouncing along; they
Love to bounce and sing
Their own song.
Frogs are so special to me;
They leap along and live so free.

Whitney Osterhout
Age: 11

THE GIRL WHO ISN'T THERE

I sit and I stare
Yes, I sit and I stare
I stare at the girl who isn't there.
I stare into darkness and I see her there
I see the girl who isn't there.
She whispers to me of joy and of glee.
I don't understand why they don't see.
She's as plain as day to me!
She's the girl who isn't there.

Pamela Levine
Age: 10

A BED FULL OF MILKY WAY

You might think the night sky is a pretty sight,
You might think it is a twinkling delight,
But, NO, it's much more it's a bed for the NIGHT.

The stars are the lights so the night won't be afraid,
The Milky Way's the sheets all carefully laid,
The moon's the night's mother singing,
With a twinkle in her eye,
The wind's the song she's singing, a sweet lullaby.

So the night goes to sleep, in it's Milky Way bed,
While the stars are twinkling softly o'er head,
And when the night awakes the daylight is shed.

Then the night gets in its bright yellow suit,
And bright yellow socks and bright yellow boots,
And night climbs a mountain and starts to fly,
And helps brighten the world, helps brighten the sky.

And on the way night meets the sun,
And much more daylight starts to come,
And then night's job is to help see there's light,
And as the day comes...
There is no more NIGHT.

Rosemary Kendrick
Age: 10

40

THE SNOW

Softly floating is the snow,
Landing wherever the wind brings,
Silently creeping around,
Calmly looking around.

The snow lands quietly,
When it lands many people make snowmen,
Laughing and giggling are the children,
Looking at the snowmen they created.

Snow, snow wherever you go,
You bring happiness to children,
So please come back another day.

Jessica Wong
Age: 13

APPLES, APPLES

Apples, apples,
I love apples,
apples, apples,
all sorts of apples,
red, yellow and green,
all sorts of colors too.
Apples, apples,
I love apples,
Yes I do, do you?

Michele M. Frix
Age: 8

41

BASEBALL

Baseball is a very fun sport.
You could never get bored of it.
There are so many things you could do in baseball.
You could make diving catches and triple plays,
You could hit grand slams and win a World Series.
Baseball is a great sport to play.

Francisco J. Rodriguez
Age: 13

MY FAT, OLD CAT

If you want to know about my cat,
I will tell you this,
He's lazy and doesn't do a thing
But after food he gives a kiss.
Oh, he's a fat, old cat
I'll tell you that.
He's as lazy as can be.
He almost looks mad a times,
But I know he still loves me.
Everyone's a sucker for him
But, yet, I just roll my eyes.
He always will play the innocent,
But I know it's just lies.
I'll tell you this,
I'll tell you that,
But I'll always love my fat, old cat.

Frances Winters
Age: 13

RACING, RUNNING

Racing, running 'round the track;
Cement makes my feet ache.
I feel sweaty, hot and sticky --
Forcing my feet to work.
One more time, just one more time 'round the track
Must I go, breathing hard terribly hard,
My throat feels dry and sore.
Halfway there, halfway there, trees and fields go by.
Gaining speed, gaining speed,
The end is very nigh.
Now I feel the cool cool water racing
Running down my throat, racing running down

Jessica Kate Feinstein
Age: 10

HUMAN NATURE

As the day moves on,
People grow and see that they are old.
Consciously they move,
From place to place,
Like wanderers in the desert.

They see that they are not alone,
But alienated from other races.
We cannot avoid the ignorance of others.

Kevin Yee
Age: 13

THE DOG

Is it a he?
Or is it a she?
Don't ask me!

Loving, giving cute too
He's a dog he doesn't say moo
Droopy eyes he looks sad
Who could ever get mad

Funny ears that hang down
It looks like he has a frown
It seems to me he ran away
We'd better help him find the way.

Margan Neumarker
Age: 10

DRAGONS

Dragons are the coolest,
I know you know it too,
But when they come to fight with you
You'll scream out 'Oh! Foo!'
Dragons have big nostrils,
Which blow big flames of fire,
But when they flame at you,
You'll really regret it too.

Tyler Kroymann
Age: 10

THE PIG

I once went to the market and met an old nag
Glasses and a hat otherwise a rag
I think he was a hog
His breath was like a heavy smog
He had a pony tail
I couldn't believe he was really for sale.
At a quarter to three
I sat down for tea
Just to find out he likes me
At that moment I couldn't believe
I bought the nag with a mighty heave
Now I'm sorry that I did because I'm poor
That pig pushed me out the door
He took up all the room in the house
Now I sleep outside with the kicked-out mouse.

Joshua Reynolds
Age: 10

SUMMER IS OVER

Silky petals falling.
A 'v' of birds softly calling.
A faraway stream, a loud trickle.
I sit with my brother, licking a popsicle.
Summer's over, that's how it looks!
School is starting.
Go get your books!

Imogen Lee
Age: 9

CLOUDS

Clouds are lumpy, clouds are bumpy,
Clouds are fluffy, clouds are puffy,
Clouds are white, clouds are bright
Clouds are steamy, clouds are dreamy.

Clouds watch the world go by,
Clouds reach out and touch the sky.
Clouds make life seem so easy
They only drift by when it's breezy.
Clouds send down buckets of rain,
That makes Saturdays seem a pain.
Clouds are the sky's coat,
For they do nothing but float.
I love clouds.

Allison White
Age: 10

HUNGRY KITTEN

A kitten jumped upon a shelf.
She was all by her hungry self.
The milk had arrived today, just now.
It had come straight from a white, old cow.
She tipped the bottle and milk poured out.
'Get off the counter!' her owner did shout.
Her owner had come to get milk in a cup.
Oh well, too bad. Kitten lapped it all up.

Kendra Kirsch
Age: 10

They are mad
They are sad
They are lost
In a block
They are weak
And they are bleak
The boy enjoys his toys
And the bear
Cared for their hair
And they ate black
Little snack
And the boy hurl
On the girl
And they miss
The big kiss.

Solen Cashman

I have a dragon named Mog.
He eats just like a hog.
He greets me like a dog.
Mog is really nice.
He's good at rolling dice.
And he wouldn't even hurt mice.
Because he's so so nice.
Did I mention he's trained like a dog?
That's my Mog.
My dragon.
And he always will be!

Jed Adler
Age: 10

This man can throw the ball
He can make a hull
To his friend who is tall
He will make the call.
He might run the ball
And make a bad call
And get tackled instead of the hull
He will probably make the hull.

Andy Lofgren
Age: 10

THE ROBIN IN THE EGG

I wonder what the world is like
Thought the robin inside the egg,
Lots of things to look at,
Watch my friends beg,
For yummy, juicy, worms,
And worms have no legs.
Trees, flowers, and fields of gold,
Standing out there, big and bold,
Lots of friends for me to make,
Then we will stand by a lake,
As we watch the birds fly by,
One suddenly catches my eye,
And he swoops down and catches his fill,
Then he rises, and rises still,
I can't wait until that day,
When I get to soar up and fly away.

Lisa Gaynon
Age: 10

THE LIFE OF A TREE

I planted a seed
The seed did not grow
Then I watered the seed
Then the seed started to grow
It started to look like a tree
Then when I forgot to water the tree it started to die
So I watched the tree a lot and then it got real big
It had some berries on it and some flowers too
A year later the tree got really old
And the berries and flowers
Did not grow on it anymore
It got all shriveled up and then a week later it died
I felt so sad and lonely that I planted a new seed

Teresa Michele Tomarchio
Age: 10

COMPUTER PUP

The curious pup, computer wiz,
Wants to finish his working biz.
From the ground, all he's seen,
Is the computer's lit up screen.
This pup's smart, smart as us beings
This pup's really a wonderful thing
Then he saw his master working
My turn he barks
Now his life is rightly perking.

Matt Tseng
Age: 10

Bugs bugs
Some are slimey
Some are silvery soft
And some are big and fat
That you don't want to look at.

Caroline Beers
Age: 9

TOGETHER AND I

As we mature and grow,
Either fast or slow,
We may look back in sorrow.
When we ponder over today and tomorrow.

I would like to see
All that I was, all I could be.
I would remember the parties, graduations.
The romances, family and friends, and expectations.
And I would remember our final celebrations.

Together we'll cry.
Together we'll laugh.
Together we'll wipe a tear from our eye.
And together we'll say good-bye.
And remember what we once were.
But, we'll march forward, together.....

Maxwell Mak
Age: 13

STAND TALL BLACK WOMEN

A hundred years you've journeyed high
from the slave shack to the hill,
of successful sons and daughters
educated and tried to fulfill

First came reading then writing
or did they come together
leading your mind every which way
through all the stormy weathers.

Striving on
with your great hope and distress,
praying it won't take two hundred years
to release the pressure off my chest.

Quietly you moved about doing what you had
mad but always kept a smile,
cleaning, ironing, standing
singing all would be right after a while

Stand tall black women you've
been through a lot,
But you still haven't hit
the deepest settling spot.

Orisha N. Parris

EVER!

Eyes open wide,
soul not inside.
Down in the gutter,
not a word does he utter.
No pain does he feel,
no hunger from missing meals.
His body begins to rot,
in that dirty old spot.
No one around,
the body not found. ever!

Jessica Lyman
Age: 15

ODE TO THE MOON

Oh, Moon!
I always wonder if the goddess
Really lives there on the moon.
Does it tickle when she walks on you?
I really like to look at you every night,
I wonder how you smell, feel, hear, and taste like?
I think you taste like a beautiful egg,
Smell like a sweet, sweet cantaloupe,
And feel slippery like a wet floor.
Oh, I love you moon.

Jacqueline Wong
Age: 8

Whom shall I blame for my mistakes?
When I don't understand a subject,
Should I blame my teacher?
When I get in a fight,
Should I blame my opponent.
Whom shall I blame,
When I can't get a job
Or get in trouble with the law?
Is it right to blame society?
Should I blame others for my mistakes?
No. I am not perfect
I must take responsibility for my mistakes.
I shall blame no one.

Leslie Richards
Age: 13

A CUTE LITTLE PUPPY

A cute little puppy all furry and brown,
He's eager and adorable
With no sign of a frown.
He's happy and playful.

This cute little puppy all floppy and young
When he opens his mouth
You'll see his red tongue
A cute little puppy.

Nicole Ling
Age: 9

                   Basketball
                   fun great
            exciting sweating playing
                a game of sweat
            running jogging passing
                 challenge spit
                    Sports

                              Zachary Ingwaldson
                              Age: 10

MY DOG

My little pal is not a cow,
And he does not meow.
He is just like me,
When he sits on my knee.
He is like a big dog,
But not a hog.
My pal is a dog,
And his fur is the color of smog.
My dog lies on a mat,
And he chews on my hat.
My dog can crawl on a ball,
But he does fall.
I don't know how he does bow,
But he can do it somehow.
He'll be my friend,
Until the end.

                              Ashley Housten
                              Age: 10

Don't mess with your brother,
    or you'll be in trouble with your mother.
Don't snack before dinner,
    or you'll be a sinner.
Don't stay up late,
    or you'll be tired at that rate.
Don't play with matches,
    or you'll burn yourself to ashes.

Jeannine Manguiat
Age: 10

THE PIG

I have a weird pig.
My pig is very big.
He is also pretty smart.
And has a huge lovable heart.
He wears tacky glasses and a straw hat.
Personally I don't like that hat.
It makes him look big and fat.
He is furry and bright pink.
When female pigs walk by
He gives them the love wink.
He thinks he's attractive.
When he snorts it's distractive.
Because he is distracting me.
We're taking a walk to the pork factory.
Tomorrow I'll have bacon for a meal.
I'm not kidding this is for real.

Chris Adams
Age: 10

TEARS

We cry with tears,
we cry with fear.
We cry when we're sad,
and even when we're glad.
We cry to our dad,
we cry to our mom.
We cry in our hands,
and even in our palms.
We cry to see,
we cry to hear,
But above all,
we cry with tears.

Bobbie Houngviengkham
Age: 14

WATER

Wet, warm and fun.
That's what water is.
You drink it, on really hot days.
You swim in it when summer comes.
Water is the best,
So excuse me but
I'm going swimming
Without telling you
The rest, ha-ha ha-ha ha!

Neta Hamou
Age: 11

SOMEONE WHO'S JUST LIKE YOU

I need someone to call my friend
When things just don't go right.
I need someone to call my friend when
I have these sleepless nights.
I need someone to call my friend
When I just don't know what to do.
I need someone to call my friend
Someone who's just like you.

Someone who's nice, sweet,
And caring- considerate too.
Someone who knows how to make me happy
When I'm down and blue.
Someone who I respect and trust
And never hold a fuss.
Someone who will share things with me
And never feels lust.

I need someone to call my friend
Right now and forever, I do.
I need someone to call my friend
Someone who's just like you.

Candace Lang
Age: 14

57

PUPPY

Puppy, puppy
No bark puppy
Red-gold, excitable,
Quick, cuddly dog.

Puppy, puppy
No bark puppy
Frisky, bouncy,
Floppy, wiggly dog.

When I take her on a walk,
She scampers here and there
Listening
To every little sound.

As I lay on the floor watching T.V.,
Her head pushes under my hand.

When she looks in the window,
She whines with her sad, brown eyes,
Floppy ears and waggly tail.

Puppy, puppy
No bark puppy
Red-gold, excitable,
Quick, cuddly dog.

Juliana Neely
Age: 12

YES CLUB

Yes Club is the answer
Yes Club is the way
If you're into ecology
Join the Yes Club today.

Youth engaged in service
That is what it means
We proudly show our tee shirts
And grubby hands and jeans.

Litter abatement and recycling is the key
Keeping the earth green and healthy
It's the only way to be- you'll see.

Athena Lynn Sjoberg
Age: 13

MY LIFE

Sometimes my life is good other times it isn't.
Sometimes it's like I have nothing to live for.
But most of the time I do.
Sometimes I want to run away.
Very few times I don't.
Sometimes I can handle my life
Very few times I can't.
Sometimes I can look so innocent.
When I'm really not.

Holly Belser
Age: 14

DON'T TELL MOM I'VE BEEN JUMPING ON MY BED

On my bed I will jump and jump and jump.
When I fall,
On my head I will bump and bump and bump.

I will run to the bathroom to hide,
So my mother won't know I cried.
I don't want my mother to know
Because she will say I told you so,

If you jump and jump and jump on your bed,
You will fall,
And bump and bump and bump your head.

Marquette Bourda & Lakeesha Calhoun

ALPHABET

Abcdefg that darn alphabet is bothering me
I hate the y I get stuck on b
I can't even pronounce the z
Abcdefg that darn alphabet really bugs me
Even the j even the c
That darn alphabet really bugs me
Abcdefgxyz next time won't you help me!

Elliott Hibbs
Age: 10

Grandparents
nice, lovable
spoiling, loving, caring
warm, huggable human beings
sharing, worrying, exciting
great, intelligent
Human Beings

Taliah N. Kirven
Age: 10

PEACE

What is peace?
Is it to hear birds singing?
Is it to be without war?
Is it to be without conflict?
What is peace?
Is it to be without stupidity?
Is it to be without racism?
Is it to be without hate?
What is peace?
Is it to be without put-downs?
Is it to love with your heart?
Is it to love with your eyes?
Or is it to love money?
And again I ask -
What is peace?
And yet no one hears me.

Jamil K Akins
Age: 13

I AM

I am a confused male
Trying to stay away from violence!
I wonder how long will I live!
I hear sirens,
I see an ambulance,
I want the violence to stop!
I am a confused male
Trying to stay away from violence!

I pretend to feel happy, although I am really sad.
I feel mad when someone is hurt or killed.
I touch God and ask that things change.
I worry that my mom and I will die
In the midst of all this violence!
I cry when someone close to me dies.
I am a confused male
Trying to stay away from violence!

I understand that some don't know any better.
I say that one day it will stop.
I dream that it will get better.
I try my best not to use violence.
I hope things will one day change.
I am a confused male
Trying to stay away from violence!

Donovan Jamil Byrd
Age: 12

My height
Short, small
Growing very secretly
Hiding very big dreams
A sleeping giant!

Timmy Van Blarigan
Age: 9

MY SPECIAL FRIEND

She's always there, to shelter me,
To give me hope, to help me see.
Her words are strong and firmly spoken.
But her promises are never broken.
Through the good times she was there,
And the bad, she helped me bear.
Her heart is gentle, caring and warm.
She led my family through many bad storms.

Whenever I was hurt, she cried too.
And when I helped someone,
Her pride shone through.
Her love was never silent or restrained,
And though life was hard, the good in her remained.

She helped me, my sister and my brother,
My special friend:
My mother.

Kyla Faison
Age: 14

My hair black and smooth.
Wary like trees in the winter.
It bounces like a ball.
Curly like Temple's.
My hair is ebony.
A frame for God's masterpiece.

Beatrice A. Flemister
Age: 9

FLY HIGH

Summer has ended.
Fall has begun.
As it swiftly soars,
through the great gray skies.
Songs of sorrows crosses my mind.

As the birds fly so high,
so high in the sky.

Going against the wind,
so strongly yet so shy.

The sun has fallen.

Stars have brightened.
The birds are gone.

Ellanora Wolfgramm
Age: 14

MY LIFE IS

My life is...
>   as new as the birth
>   of a newborn baby.

My life is...
>   as smooth as a pencil
>   as it glides across paper.

My life is...
>   like waves crashing
>   against the seashore.

My life is...
>   as joyful as witnessing
>   a baby's first step.

My life is...
>   as awesome as
>   a roller coaster ride.

My life is...
>   like a runner sprinting
>   for the finish line.

Thank you God that my life is...

Monica J. Green
Age: 9

THE FRUITS OF LIFE

I cram in the succulents
of spring's beloved fruits
the sea-green apples,
the scarlet strawberries.
As I gnaw this juicy pulp
I imagine the beautiful places
I have seen in my existence
upon this dot in the far corner
of this shining galaxy.
I see the crimson magnolias
spotted with transparent dew,
the deep cool forget-me-not blue lagoons
which I bathe in without care
as I savor and digest
the fruits of my life.

Argenta Walther
Age: 10

My dog
black, white
never very bright
walks, sleeps, eats
doesn't like to stay on his feet
a fluffy white and black ball
not real tall
a friend that no one has
he is always a little glad.

Sarah Peterson
Age: 9

THE DAY HE WAS ALIVE

That day I saw him.
He lay there, crying forever.
Through hard and happy hours,
We wished he could talk.
His scent was sweet and fresh.
He looked like a raspberry.
His eyes opened, wide with surprise.
That day everyone cried, happy with joy.
Now, he has locks of curly dark-brown hair.
He has eyes that look intently
For mischievous wonders,
A laugh which lights his face up with happiness.
A body with chubby limbs.
My big-little brother George.

Stephanie Morabe
Age: 12

V.I.P.

Michael Jordan
fearless, positive, determined
number 23 in his red and black uniform
is preparing to slam, jump, fly, and 'juk'
his way to the hoop
on any basketball court
this is one player that truly deserves to be called
'Air'

Corey N. Harper
Age: 12

There is no love here anymore
It has been long before,
Before anyone could see,
See how much it has hurt me

Now this part of me is killed
And it can't be fulfilled

There is no love here anymore
He has left only a sore
That hurts me even more,
Than before

This person died
Which made me cry

Now he is nothing more but
A memory which lives in me

There is no love here anymore.

Alexandria White
Age: 11

C   hocolate colors they may be,
A   nd maybe even orange,
T   hey could be black, they could be white,
S   o if you see a blue one that would be quite a sight.

Jenna Roberts
Age: 11

Perched on a tree,
There I see, I see a bird.
A bird of grace, a bird of wondrous heights
Its flight, soaring above,
Many others dream of the sight this bird can see.
But I am happy this bird is free.

Nora Hammer
Age: 13

ALONE

I am alone in a world that is cold
no one cares no one dares to even
share a kind word or gesture.

I am alone in ways I cannot
explain but I can feel through
pain and sorrow.

I am alone and I am hurt I swallow
my pain through smiles by day and
tears by night.

I am alone no one understands the
way I feel and just maybe they don't
care but I say to myself I am alone
but I am FREE!!!

Naima Mayes
Age: 13

COLORS COLORS

Colors, colors, what a beautiful sight;
Colors, colors, might they be bright;
Colors, colors, might they be blue;
Colors, colors, are on my shoes;

Colors, colors, are all around;
Colors, colors are on the ground;
Colors, colors, are in the sky;
Colors, colors, are very shy;

Colors, colors, are everywhere;
Colors, colors, there are lots to share;
Colors, colors, are in my room;
Colors, colors, are on a broom;

Colors, colors, are on the floor;
Colors, colors, oh how I adore!
Colors, colors, are above;
Colors, colors, are like a dove;

Colors, colors, the Lord has made;
Colors, colors, are like a parade;
Colors, colors, red and blue;
Colors, colors, stick like glue;

Colors, colors, orange and green;
Colors, colors, are like a machine;
Colors, colors, are in my head;
Colors, colors, will never be dead;

Colors, colors, are like a parachute;

Colors, colors, can be cute;
Colors, colors, pink and gray;
Colors, colors, will never fade away.

Taneaca C. Tatum
Age: 12

DON'T STOP! DON'T GIVE UP NOW!

Don't stop! Don't give up now!
Keep on striving
Because for centuries and centuries
Our ancestors fought
To get us to where we are today.

So Don't stop! Don't give up now!
Keep pushing higher and higher
Don't let anything stop you
Or get in your way.

So when that road gets tough
And you are thinking about giving up
Don't, just reach toward the top
Let people know who you really are
You are somebody!

Don't stop, keep on going
Keep right on going!

Tamberlyn Latrice Crayton
Age: 13

Myself
active and strong
working, pumping, and feeling
on Earth, third planet from the Sun
friendly, gentle, and kind

Ragnar Christian Svare
Age: 9

NIGHT OF THE BOBCAT

I am fast, sly, and sleek,
I see a river I take a drink.
I see the night coming from behind the sun,
I have to hurry, I start to run.
I look for my dinner,
It is in the center of my path.
I strike it with all my might,
I always did kill better at night.
Ha! My dinner 'was' a rabbit fast and free,
Once I grabbed it I ate with glee.
Time for me to sleep,
I run home without a peep.
I now climb my tree,
I found the spot, it was warm not hot.
For now my day is finished,
Now I nap.
For I am the bobcat.

Christopher Michael Hastay
Age: 11

WISHES

I write of people who
are lonely and poor,
I write of people who
are rich and content.
I think about how
different peoples' lives
are, from one person
to another.

If I had a wish, I'd
wish that nobody was
every poor, and that
everybody lived happy
lives, where nobody
had to be tortured in
wars, and end their
lives in misery.

At night, people clasp
their hands in prayer,
hoping that someday
people will live happy
peaceful lives, but alas,
our wishes have not yet
been granted.

Courtncy T. Little
Age: 12

AIN'T NO SUNSHINE

In the ghetto there's no sunshine,
All there is in the ghetto is black out.
People in the ghetto can make sunshine
if they all try to get along and live together.
I would at least like to see sunshine
at least once in a while.
But can I, no.
All I see is people fighting and killing each other.
If we all get along we would see the sunshine
in the ghetto.
Ain't no sunshine where I go.
All I see is crack babies, drugs,
and most of all violence that will not stop
unless people start thinking what they're doing.
Ain't no sunshine where you go or I go.
But we can make one if we try.

Lorena Mora
Age: 13

BLACK

People are so jealous of the delicate black skin,
So natural and so pure.
All throughout the body so rich and so sweet.
No one wants to realize or even see
How beautiful it is to be black and blessed,
Full of elegance.

Jacquelynn Renee Robinson
Age: 13

74

AT THE END OF THE ROAD

At the end of the road,
hope awaits me.
It seems like a short walk,
but God can only tell.
As I walk
visions of going home
flash through my mind,
but I know I must go on
and live out my dream.
As thirsty as the desert and
as tired as a drunken old man
I walk down the path
to get to the end of the road.
My belly is growling like a fighting lion
and the hot sun burns my skin,
my heart is pounding like a drum,
but soon the end would come.
Day and night I walk,
soon I come to the end of the road.
A bright light is at the end
and now I know I made it
I made it to the end of the road.

Naseema McElroy
Age: 12

A MARTIAN SENDS A POSTCARD HOME

They stuff these white, fluffy animals
with brown liquid on top, into a hole in their heads.
Sound comes out of that hole.

They cover their world with big blue sheets
that have a big ball on it, and it also has
those small animals on it.
But the animals that they put on those sheets
are hundreds of times larger.

As soon as the world gets darker
they take away that big ball and replace it
with another ball that is white and dirty
and sometimes you can only see half of it.
They add tiny sparkly things to it.

They have the strangest creatures on Earth.
Its top is green and its long bottom
is brown with tiny cracks.
The humans protect themselves by ripping off
the creatures' arms once in a while.
They also make paper out of those creatures.

Humans have long skinny little worms on their head
which they sometimes let creatures with 2 eyes eat.
Or they sometimes let these creatures
with lots of teeth eat or smooth out their worms.
They let so many different sorts of creatures
eat their worms.

Earth is such a strange but interesting planet.
The people here are strange and the things are too.
You should come visit Earth.

It's so much different than our planet.

Love,
Jun

Sovanna Yorn
Age: 12

A MARTIAN SENDS A POSTCARD HOME

So here I am, Water World is what my friends call it.
But when I landed, there was no water in sight.
And so wandering around
Looking at the artificial cotton in the sky.
Then I stopped to ponder, and said, 'Where am I?'.
Then I saw a horrifying monster, with big glass eyes
And 10 or 20 swinging mouths,
Some humans risked being eaten up,
But some managed to get out.
So I decide to go in
And see the big monster that said vacancy.
When I went in the monster's mouth
I saw a figure with humans trapped inside it.
Then I saw a long cushion.
I stood on it and then I started to hop
Without myself making movement.
So I stopped, laid down, closed my eyes
And began to snore.

Bory Kas
Age: 12

I AM

I am Karis. I have Indian, White and Black all in me.
I am wild and strange.
I wonder how the living things were before I was born.
I hear echoes everywhere.
I think my shadow is an echo.
I see rain, fog, smog. I see blood dripping from a lion.
I see aliens on the moon.
I want freedom and peace.
I am Karis. I have Indian, White and Black in me.
I am wild and strange.

I pretend I am a Coyote in the moon.
I fly past the moon. I am a ghost and an alien.
I feel spirit in me and life. I carry love in my touch.
I touch the fur on my dog's skin, I touch ghosts.
I worry about the world. I worry about the galaxy.
I cry when I hear my echo blow.
I am Karis. I have Indian, White and Black all in me.
I am wild and strange.

I understand my dog and my spirit.
I say strange things like, 'Home is the world creative.'
I dream about being a coyote.
I try to imagine being a coyote.
I hope I can go to Russia.
I am Karis. I have Indian, White and Black all in me.
I am wild and strange.

Karis Anne Daggs
Age: 9

A MOTHER'S LOVE

A mother's love is sent from God above.
A mother takes care of you
So you won't have a cold or flu.
A mother helps you do your hair.
A mother will always be there.
A mother teaches you to get A's and B's.
A mother teaches you to say thank you and please.
A mother is filled with lots of love.
A mother teaches not to push or shove.
A mother is very helpful,
Therefore treat her back with lots of love.
That is a mother's love.

Trymica N. Provost
Age: 12

LONELINESS

I enter the forest,
Dark, deep, and lonely.
A chasm of silence falls.
The rustling of trees stopped.
The howling of wolves stopped.
And the birds song stopped too.
I feel lonelier than when
I entered.

Nimia Barrera
Age: 12

I LIKE MUSIC

I like music,
I can play good
So don't trip;

Music is my thang,
I like to rap and my
Raps ain't the same;

I like jazz and blues,
Everybody knows I'm cool;

I can play music cause
I'm talented,
I can't help it,
'Cause that's what I'm born with.

Ayikwei Scott
Age: 12

THE WORLD AROUND US

Sometimes it is nice to think
About the world around you
About the wonders and joys
And the laughter it employs
And the love in the air
That surrounds you

Max Anderson
Age: 12

AM I NOT

Am I not the glistening glow of a child,
Am I not the laugher of the children at play.
Am I not the heroes time just passed,
Am I made of steel and not glass.
Am I not the summers and winters time just passed.
Or am I a happy ending of a great story.
Am I not a smile that brightens everyone's day.
Or am I a hot burning light on San Fransico's highway.
Am I not the joy in everyone's heart
Or just families that seem to part.

I am but, I still ask myself
Am I not.

Rose Jonielle Smoot
Age: 12

BROWN

The taste of chocolate fudge
The sound of an old fishing boat leaving harbor
Fall and cinnamon, and freshly burned firewood
Smells brown
Brown is dirt
Brown is the color of my skin
Brown is a fireplace, cinnamon,
And an old fishing boat leaving harbor.

Carl Jahi Williams, III.
Age: 10

My dog
big, nice
fun, jumpy, funny
usually a good girl
Mishka

Jonathan Van Selow
Age: 10

BLACK POWER

Black Power: means pride in my Black Heritage,
pride in my Black Parents.

Black Power: means a richer, healthier life.

Black Power: means better education and a
meaningful job.

Black Power: means a desire to change from the
way things are now.

Black Power: means holding on to our land.

Black Power: does not mean anarchy; it is not
communist plot by outside agitators.

Black Power: means: LIFE

Sylvia Davis
Age: 13

A RED CHRISTMAS BALL

Plump.
But pretty, like a red Christmas ball.
Hanging on to love,
Just floating there,
Waiting to fall and shatter.

Jennifer Tan
Age: 11

MY HOUSE OF DREAMS

Once I dreamed of a romantic house
That was a house on the ocean spray
My house of dreams
It could be in the moon's glory
With emphasis on the wave's shimmering breeze
On the cool night in a full moon.
Lays my house with excellent movement of passion,
His eyes glittered and his voice grew sharp with scorn.
And happy to be
A chance to be me
My house of dreams
I dream of a night of romantic ocean view
If there's something I want
I will create a real home of dreams
Where would it be?
'Ocean sunset night'
My house of dreams.

Alba Alberto
Age: 12

TO RIDE THE WIND

I have heard men
  Known as Nobles
  Say they
  Will ride upon the wind

I have heard women
  Known as Ladies
  Say they
  Will ride upon the wind

I have heard children
  Of all shapes and sizes
  Say they
  Will ride upon the wind

As yet though, it has not happened
  For, to do so
Their desire, and knowledge
  Must reach new levels
  Never before achieved
  Or, in fact, even thought of
Time will tell
  Soon we will know
  If I can
  If anyone can
  Or will
Ride upon the wind

Emily Vartanian
Age: 12

S   pring comes once a year,
P   lease, like it's something to hear,
R   ain comes during springtime.
I   t'll probably cancel recess time.
N   o wonder I really like summer,
G   ee, what a bummer.

Antonio Wong-Carrillo
Age: 10

TIME

The clock ticks,
my heart beats,
my eyes wander,
the chair squeaks,
the bell rings,
the door creaks.

Melissa Cahn
Age: 14

THANKSGIVING

This Thanksgiving
Pilgrims, pumpkins, pudding
Wondering, pondering...
All means something to me.
But what is it?
I don't really know.
The gold, the flowers
It's all so new to me.
Roosters, all look so pretty.
I'm pondering...
The birds, church, life,
It's all related to nature.
It's coming to me it's
Thankfulness.

Christopher Lim
Age: 9

THE FIERCE TORNADO

A tornado goes round and round
Making lots of sound!
Better run,
Better get away,
The tornado is spining your way!
The tornado is fierce, not much fun,
Get away, run run!

Matthew Rubinstein
Age: 10

THE NEW DAY

Here comes a day that we haven't begun
In a world that you can't get by unless you're the one,
The brains, the smarts, the ultimate wise
Your I.Q. is as high as the skies
In the new day, it's true, any thing can happen
But you have to be quiet so quit your yappen!
In the new day, all you need are dreams
Or so to me it seems.

Mario Camacho
Age: 13

LIVELY NATURE

Lively leaves at my feet,
  Blowing in the wind.
Lively leaves red and brown,
  Lively leaves on the ground.
Lively trees, way up high
  Blowing in the wind.
Lively trees green and brown
  Lively trees tall and round.
Lively nature's everywhere
  Trees and leaves astound,
Lively nature's beautiful
  With flowers all around!

Joshua Willey
Age: 9

STRANDED

I sink into the sand
As I watch the sunset
The cool waves kiss my feet
And the breeze
Runs it's fingers through my hair
As my love disappears over the horizon
I pray that it will return to me
When morning comes
And I will no longer be alone.

Laura Heywood
Age: 14

This is a warning your parents
Have told you over and over again.
You better look both ways
Before you cross the street
You might think you're fast
You might think you're lucky
But you aren't made of steel
And you might just slip on a banana peel
And wind up stuck to a big fat wheel
And little boys and girls
This is NOT a very good deal.
So could you look both ways
Before you cross the street.

Jeremiah Kincannon
Age: 10

DUST

The tide slowly drifts inwards,
bringing with it love.
As the tide dissipates,
it seems as though
a part of you
has gone with it.
When the tide comes in,
it bring with it
many things;
rocks,
seaweed,
shells,
and bones.
Bones which speak of the past
in their own strange way.
The past,
which you wish you
could bring back,
all the while
knowing that the tide
could never recover it.
Where has that love gone?
Have the currents swept it faraway,
like the sliver of the moon
that becomes full,
and in time, fades away?
The tide still goes in and out,
just as the sun rises and sets,
but now your love is coming in with
the tide somewhere else.

Sarah Threlfall
Age: 13

WISHES

Don't you ever wish that you were eating a dish,
It probably wouldn't taste too good,
It would be better than wood,
Wouldn't you like to have a bird,
Even if it could only say one word,
Have you ever heard the word one-third?
I think it seems so absurd,
When I think of the word line,
I get a chilly feeling down my spine,
I wish I had a furry cat,
But not one very, very, fat,
I'd hate to have a frog or toad,
Because they'd probably explode,
When I'm in my car and going around a bend,
I have a feeling it's The End!

Briana Williford
Age: 9

TO LOVE YOUR SHOES

Shine your shoes with a friend
Let it look shiny
Do not step in the mud
Or you will have to shine it again
You must be kind to them
You must step in them softly

Gaow Michelle Suwannukul
Age: 12

THE RIVER

It bubbles and gurgles
As it spills over the rim
It churns and turns as
A thrashing dragon that cannot swim.

The waters are rough as
It takes in the rain
Swirling and turning as
It it's in pain.

It flows onto the land
To make people run
You can see it laugh
As if it's having fun.

People flee crying 'dear me'
But the water keeps going on
Having no mercy for those beyond.

Then all comes to a subtle end
The water resigns back to its vein
The swirling the turning
The churning the gurgling and
The bubbling it has all stopped
It's now calm once again.

As was the floods of the Mighty Mississippi, 1993.

Alexis Charles
Age: 10

91

THE BEAUTIFUL WAVES

From Scotties Bluff
you could see the waves,
Going through
and out the caves.
I watch them crash and splash
against the rocks,
As they give me
surprising shocks.
I will never forget
how we were tough,
When we climbed
up Scotties Bluff.

Christina Dang
Age: 10

MY LOVE

I have climbed the highest
mountains crossed the deepest
seas and walked the hottest
desert to find you.

But my love you weren't there.
Where have you been all my
life? My Love.

Sonya Jubb
Age: 12

On towering cliffs above,
One oak stands alone.
Mighty yet weak as it dangles off the cliff.

Nat Miller
Age: 11

ONLY THE ETERNAL

I'm thinking of a creature who once ruled the land,
Who once ruled the land, long before man.
Some would walk, some would soar,
This creature is called the 'Dinosaur'.
We have no one to blame for their absence today,
Only the Eternal who took them away.
'Were they replaced by mankind?
Will mankind be replaced?'
Only the Eternal knows.
So don't worry about a doomsday, that is the future,
And only the Eternal knows.

Jack Isaac Dresnick
Age: 10

THOUGHTS RISING

Gurgling over
spilling down
tumbling, fumbling
turning around.
Bubbling up to the surface,
trickling out of a spout,
into a whisper or even a shout.

Putting pen to paper-
twirling it about,
somehow the words of poems
just come out.

Alexis Sclamberg
Age: 11

THE TREE

There was a tree in my backyard
It filled me with glee no matter what the regard.
Shady by day and cozy at night
My tree kept me away from fright.

Birds shared this tree with me
And lots of other animals, some very pesky.
Worms would crawl in and out of the leaves
I sure hope my tree never gets cleaved.

Ryan Odell
Age: 10

OAKLAND

Where the day is bent by no one man's birth or death
Where sound never stops
Here the population only rises
This city with its every breath of air
Has diverse imagination and spirit
With its every face a blend of nations
With its every arm cradling a modern atmosphere
In its every street lies the old traditions of architecture
And the new cultural ethics

A world lacking guidance and nurturing
Lays beneath the city's shell
A world where drugs and violence
Deaden the future of many one by one
Generation by generation
As rapidly as the population grows
Life for many darkens

This city shall one day fill the gap
In the lives of its people
This city shall cope with the ups and downs
As it expands endlessly
This city shall hold its diversity close to it
As there shall be a great difference in every man
Though this difference none shall see.

Cassandra Compton
Age: 12

COLOR SENSE

Pink
The color pink smells like a rosebud
   just begging to open.
The color pink is how I feel
   when I am really happy.
Pink looks like a person holding their breath
   for a long time.
The color pink tastes like
   strawberry pop-tarts with pink frosting.
Pink sounds like the fire crackling
   in our living room on a cold winter night.

Isabelle Boone

MY VOICE

My voice
is as pretty as a singer.
   My voice
sounds like a tweety bird chirping in the morning.
   My voice
is like the Little Mermaid.
   My voice
is as loud as the roaring wind.
   My voice
is like Princess Jasmine.

LaShontae Trainor
Age: 9

I AM

I am a shark who likes to swim
I wonder how people live like this
I hear the sounds of hat and hunger
I see the people living in the streets
I want to help them but I can't
I am a shark who likes to swim

I pretend I am ruler of the earth
I touch people's hearts sometimes when
I read them a poem
I worry about people dying
I cry when I hurt inside but not outside
I am a shark who likes to swim

I understand how people feel
I say I'll make it okay
I dream of being a master of disguise
I try to help other people
I hope for $999,999.99 of money
I am a shark who likes to swim

Nicholas Brown
Age: 9

SILVER

Silver
It makes me think
of a cool crystal sky
Like after a rainy
day went by.
In the city on top
of a hill
It makes everything
look quiet and still.
It makes me happy
for I like a cool day
It makes me feel
like I could just fly away.
To give up rainy
days is something I'd never
I wish I could keep
this moment forever.

T'sera Mingst-Belcher

SOMETIMES

Sometimes I like to be alone
And look up in the sky
And think my thoughts inside my head
Just me, myself, and I.

Elliot Edgemon
Age: 8

THE LAST DAYS IN MAY

On a rainy day
I spent a lot of time thinking
Thinking about the goal I set in my life
And try to remember the last days in May
Before summer lay claim
White clouds float by
Like high cotton
Back in the school yard
We made up a game
Now is always
Always the same
Too bad always always ends
Now that we're tall
And all grown
A life a mind lives of our own
I always remember the last days in May

Charles Lau
Age: 15

MY KITTEN

Kitten
rusty, white
plays, sleeps, eats
rusty, white little ball
My own little alive stuffed animal

Nicole Girard
Age: 10

THE UNITED STATES

Dreaming to a new place - United States
Flowing across oceans
Separating from relatives and families
Cry, cry, cry
Hard to say good-bye
Arriving
Afraid of speaking
Meet stranger
Going strange places
People in different cultures
People speaking different languages
Parents work hard
Hopelessly for children
Goals for having cars, house, etc....
Planning for the future

Xuemei Guan
Age: 14

FRIENDS

Friends are good to have you know.
They make you happy when you're sad.
They play with you when you're not mad.
They help you when you're having trouble.
And you need them whether
You think so or not.

Jocelyn Reid
Age: 10

MIDNIGHT DARK

Midnight Dark
so soft so sweet,
it smells like new mint
that's just been brought.
The moon so white
and the sky so dark,
O-boy, I wish I can
go out in the
Midnight Dark.

Chenille Campbell
Age: 12

STORMS IN THE SKY

As I lay in my room
I can hear the rain,
   crashing against the windows.
Everything is quiet,
   but the sky.
The claps of thunder
   shake the ground.
The sky is lit up by
   the bolts of lightning.
All is peaceful as
   I fall asleep.

Laura Sage
Age: 12

BLACK WOMAN

With my big lips
And my wide hips,
With my broad shoulders
And my nappy hair,
I see heritage, grace,
And uncontrollable power.
When my feisty face
Parades around the streets, people think,
'What a woman, what a woman.'
With big bones and a big forehead,
I stand out from the rest.
My roaring mouth shows intelligence.
With thick eyebrows and dark flesh,
I stand up with finesse.
For I am the Proud Black Woman!

Bianca Araya
Age: 13

MARIN HEADLANDS

Upon the peak of Scotty's Bluff
You see the Salty Sea.
As the wind blows through
Your hair and the sand
Into the sea
As a red tail hawk glides overhead
And the little pond flows.

Tom Phelps
Age: 10

DARKNESS

I remember being a kid and saying,
'I'm afraid of the dark.
That's when monsters, and creatures,
And ghosts come out.'
Darkness represents sad and gloomy times.
Like 'a dark and stormy night.'
It scares children out of their little minds.
Yet, to me it is a relaxer
It makes me very calm,
And makes the atmosphere around very quiet.
To some, darkness is the shadow of death,
To me, it is a symbol of serenity.

Christopher Reynolds
Age: 13

There is a deep love rising,
    Over the ashes,
    Over the fire,
    Over the house,
    From the soul.

The things I look back on now as sad,
    Are all just
    A lesson in life,
    Too hard for me to understand.

Nina Frank
Age: 10

I AM

I am the daughter of farm workers,
immigrants, maids, Spanish conquerors,
Indians, slave owners, Aztecs,
hard workers and drug addicts

I have seen my father work hard
so my sisters and I can have a good education
the education that their people never had.
He want us to have a better life
because here in 'EL Norte' life is hard

I have heard my mother cry for a solution
to the problems we have
so we can be a united family.
She has worked for a better tomorrow for us.

My family came as immigrants by foot
crossing rivers and mountains
coming to 'El Norte' for a better life.

I am the future I must work hard
for my beliefs like my parents did
I must struggle for my people
like Caesar Chavez did!

Joanna N. Garcia
Age: 14

TIGERMAN (MY LEGEND)

Once upon a time not long ago,
It was a man who lived life real slow.
But he could do things no one can,
That's when he becomes Tigerman.
Now, I want to tell you a story what 2 people did,
And tell you how Tigerman got them rid.
Now, there were two guys named Rob and Hank,
They walked into a building and robbed a bank.
But Tigerman walked in and caught them in the act,
And told those robbers to 'Put it down Jack.'
Before Tigerman left the police came,
And the police told Tigerman
'You put us to shame.'
So if you think that you can sin,
Beware of the man named Tigerman.

Derrick LeRay Abram
Age: 12

BULLFROG

The bulging throat pulsated in and out.
Its little eyes wandered around its eye sockets.
The tongue shot out and caught a fly.
The hind legs powerfully pushed the body airborne,
Onto another stepping stone.
The creek was so clear,
Its ugly reflection was seen perfectly.

Cathryn Laszlo
Age: 11

THE SNAKE

Small, slithery and sly creature.
Ancient predator slithers.

His prey, unknowing
the reptile is watching him.
His small body slithers against
the ground, hissing
Prey suddenly gets restless
Snake circulates and
ready to attack
He reaches for his food and finally...

SNATCH!!!

Isidro Garcia
Age: 13

THREE LITTLE LEAVES

Three little leaves fall softly to the ground
Orange, yellow and red
When the wind catches them
They go flying through the air.
Four little leaves fall softly to the ground
Orange, yellow, brown and red
Making a cover on the ground.

Molly McClary
Age: 6

ICE CREAM IN THE MEADOW

I'm sitting in a meadow green.
I like my ice cream round and clean.
The flavor is as sweet as a dove.
Oh ice cream, ice cream that I love!

Maura Fitzgerald
Age: 7

WHAT I SEEM TO BE

Am I what I seem to be?

The sky is blue
The sea is green
But am I what I seem to be.

Yes dogs do bark
And cats meow
But what's hidden behind my frown.

The children laugh
The children play
But am I like the sunshine of day.

If I could change one thing about me
It wouldn't bc the way I seem to be.

Vanessa Mag
Age: 12

OH MS. MOON

Oh Ms. Moon give my your light
Oh Ms. Moon shine bright tonight.
Though you're so tiny give it your best
Shine for the bird in his little nest.
Shine bright for the chipmunk scared in his tree.
Shine for me as scared as he.
Oh Ms. Moon give me your light
Oh ms. Moon shine bright tonight.

Polly Gordon
Age: 9

ASIANS

Short, small, slanted eyes
That's all they call us.

It's not true,
If you know what I mean.

It is painful to hear
I could kill them in my dreams.

I don't need to listen
Because I don't care.
I'll never care.

I am only important!!!

Hue Tran
Age: 13

YELLOW AND GREEN PLAID

The night was cold, the wind whistling
Stopping at the front door.
Inside everybody was getting ready for cozy beds.
Then out he came from the bathroom door,
His feet like triangles and his legs like twigs.
He was dressed with an approval
Except for the yellow and green plaid golf socks
He had rolled up to his knee cap.
The socks he had dared to wear.

Anjali Dharan
Age: 11

LITTLE SILKWORM

Little silkworm,
If you please,
You have all the mulberry leaves.
Make cocoons as white as milk,
And we'll make clothes of purest silk.

Sarah Fong
Age: 7

MORNING'S PREY

The deer in masses
trample the brush
in the dawn's rays
unaware of man
they brush past him
leaving their mark
for all others to see

The two worlds collide
every morning at dawn

Man goes to every corner
in search of them
but comes back
empty handed
while they lament their woes
the prey prance aloofly
right under their noses.

Justin Matis
Age: 13

White, Black, Mexican, and others
Peal off our skin, we are the same
Look at our veins, we have all the same
Look at our bodies, we all are the same
And we're all the same color when the lights go out

Gerald Polk
Age: 14

Thanksgiving
Giving, Sharing, Thanks,
Turkey, Cranberry Sauce,
Indians, Feasting, Talking
Rejoicing, Celebrating The Harvest,
Thanksgiving.

Joel Orkin-Ramey
Age: 10

WHAT IS THANKSGIVING?

I ask myself,
What is Thanksgiving?
Is it a time for self giving?
Is it a time for get togethers
Is it one of our put togethers

I look it up-
And what do I see?
How it was made-
Like a key

Finally I see
What is means to me
What it means to be
Not a Pilgrim to cross the sea

But the thanks of you and me
Just to be.

Samantha Neureuther
Age: 10

UNDER THE SEA

Underwater
Strands of pearls,
Purple green,
Flying fish,
Dancing waves so green and blue
Just so nice
Just like you.

Ella Hochhausen Marcantonio
Age: 7

I CANNOT GO OUTSIDE TODAY

I cannot go outside today.
A lion's waiting by the door.
Two six feet gorillas
Are playing tug of war.

An elephant and a tiger
Are wearing mother's coats and hats.
Mrs. Mim and Merlin the Magician.
Are discussing cats and bats.

A giant and Godzilla
Are sword fighting on the garden wall.

So, as you see, I cannot
Go outside at all.

Dana Creek
Age: 9

AFTER THE RAIN

The air is wet, and the dew is soft.
My coat is on, and my scarf has a strange taste,
Like oatmeal.
Cold air is rushing in at me like quickly moving planes.
The air is humid, like sticky honey,
Humid and cold, yet sunny.
I see the air moving, its great density
Struggling to push by.
At 6:55 AM, I'm on my way to the bus stop,
New school clothes are comfy and warm,
Fitting loosely on my chilly body.
My nose is tingling, making me shiver.
The air is set for a new day,
Wet and musty, yet refreshing and mild.
Huge trees are looming over me,
Like unwelcome guests.
Then I slightly mess up the piles
Of soggy, muddy leaves.
There's no use for people to rake, I realize,
For little leaf-blankets will never stop falling.
As I scan through each immense leaf pile,
I see the ruby and fiery, rusty and maroon leaves,
But my favorites are the crimson leaves.
My bus is here; I have to go to school.

Hillary Oyer
Age: 11

FALLING LEAVES

I watch the leaves drift to the ground,
And, I notice their radiant colors.
I can see the morning dew on the leaves
As if they are crying because of parting from the tree.
The leaves of rusty red, yellow ocher
And bronze light up the sky like the sun.
But alas, the last leaf has fallen to Earth.
Now, the trees look dull and dead.

Erin Y. Kodama
Age: 11

JUST A COLOR...

I run,
Holding to Mamma's sweaty but soft hand.
I feel like screaming letting out my anger
But I keep it in my bottle.
Let them be us for a day
See how much pain is included.
We're no different
Because it's just a color.
You should not take us as a slimy piece of trash
Being passed on to other hands,
For raining money.
But for a man like you,
We're no different, not at all
It's just a bloody color.

Claire Baker
Age: 10

LIFE IS COOL

Life is cool because
there is a lot to accomplish.

You can accomplish it by going to school
graduating
and going on to the next level.

You might want to be a star in life.

Life can also be bad, but it is your choice
to be successful in life.

Things you need to be successful:

graduate
get a job
don't be poor.

If you choose bad ways of life
you probably will never be anything.
Just a bum.
On the street.

LaShaun Allen
Age: 13

JESSICA DAVIS

Jessica
Kind, caring, cute.
Sister of Brendan
Lover of Mom, Dad, and Brother
Who feels strongly about good writing,
Computers, and environment.
Who needs private journal, food, clothes
Who gives pens, rubber bands and advice
Who fears diving boards
Would like to see Europe
A resident of San Rafael, California.
Davis

Jessica Davis
Age: 10

SPRING

Spring is a season beautiful and clear
Blooming flowers lovely dear
Bears out of hibernation ready to eat
Plump berries ripening-what a wonderful treat
Snow is melting into a stream
Salmon are coming in a shimmering gleam
Sunlight creeping in the trees
Birds are chirping out of the breeze
All these treasures come to an end
When tree cutters chop down our magical friend

Livia Shmavonian
Age: 10

THE COAST

The coast is a peaceful, playful place.
Its waves play in the mist.
  As we think of the coast we feel
The coolness of the sand, the sea, the rocky cliffs.
  As we go to the coast we feel
The sand rummages through our toes
  As the wind pushes it away.
The coast - a peaceful, playful thing.

Lisa Gordon

ALYSSA VILLA

Alyssa
Nice, flexible, caring
Sister of Ashley and Ashton
Lover of gymnastics, Sister and Mom
Who feels strongly about my health,
Kindness, sharing
Who needs money, friends, a car
Who gives toys, food, and clothes
Who fears Brother, Grandma, and spiders
Would like to see Jamaica
A resident of San Rafael, California
Villa

Alyssa Vella
Age: 9

This is a poem where everything flows,
The werds like they iz cuz thatz how it gowz,
I'll make it as long as long can be,
It's a gushing liquid poem, you'll see,
Most poems have meaning, direction, a purpose,
But mine is just meaningless, mindless verses,
This is a poem where anything goes,
Look at those toes they're Longfellows,
No tune, but this poem's a lullaby,
Sit back and relax, and always ask why,
The words work with one another together,
Working together in this endeavor,
Why write a poem that's different and new?
Because I can, I wonder can you?
Venture to let your mind be free,
Look a bit closer and see what you see,
This is a poem that does what it will,
It's running to freedom, it never stands still,
Liquid language flows in my stream,
It's free and different, it lets itself dream,
An apple sits in front of me,
Faraway from its comfy tree,
I ask it the same question I ask you,
Can you think for yourself, think something new?
Whaddooyoo care if I think out loud?
Too many of you are just part of the crowd,
Veni, vidi, vici, I came to see and ate,
I have to wait, I'm not thinking straight,
Now my poem's at medium length,
And at the midpoint it's gathering strength,
You'd never know I've creative flair,
Not a smart mouthed kid with messy hair,
I feel that I could make a stand,

Change the world with pen in hand,
I spew forth waves of lead and ink,
I scarcely ever stop to think,
If the word rhymes, or if the beat slows,
In my poem that naturally flows,
Although I'm very careful not,
To speak two times what I once thought,
What if we're all just living to die?
Or everything left in the blink of an eye?
Do you ever question reality?
Because you know you should, you see,
What if I read this poem to y'all?
Would your image of me just crumble and fall?
This is a poem that thought it could fly,
It glided, and flew, and fell from the sky,
It's a good thing this poem landed on me,
Someone else would have let it be.

Toby Wincorn
Age: 13

THE COAST

C old
O tter
A lgae
S and
T an

Daniel Wootton

MONSTERS

I like monsters.
Monsters are big
and scary,
but I say
they look like
a cherry!!!

Richard Anderson
Age: 10

THE FOOD I HATE THE MOST

I hate banana twirl, swine and swirl,
dumpster, lumpster, icky whirl.
Day old diaper, dirty windshield wiper.
Yucky, mucky, ficky, sticky, very rocky, very icky.
Used Band-Aid mosquito crunch.
Not what I would choose to munch.
Broken watch band, dirty cake pan,
smelly socks and Goldie's locks.
Eraser shavings, cement pavings, moldy wheat bread,
insect abdomen, thorax and head.
Monster hair and dino brains.
Ant filled cupcakes, acid rain.
Don't sound too good to eat?
To munch?
Well, that's what's in today's school lunch.

Catherine John
Age: 10

CHRISTMAS

Christmas is a time for Santa and presents.
HO HO HO
Christmas is a time for eating candy canes.
HO HO HO
Christmas is for skating and caroling.
HO HO HO
Christmas is a time for decorating trees.
HO
HO
HO

Andrea Chan
Age: 10

EVAN PAUL ROMANO

Evan
Funny, smart, nice,
Brother of Derek,
Lover of skiing and running.
Who feels strongly about reusing or recycling.
Paul
Who needs friends, clothes, shelter
Who gives presents, pets and toys.
Who fears robbers, crooks, kidnappers
Would like to see Europe Italy.
A resident of San Rafael, California.
Romano

Evan Romano
Age: 9

121

WAVES

The coast is empty,
the sun shows first light of day.
The water shines like crystal.
The mountains loom overhead,
silent watchers,
as the waves roll in.

The wind blows light,
the breeze is calm.
On this hot summer day,
the beach fills up with happy children,
as the waves roll in.

The people shout,
and laugh and play.
Along the shore,
they have their fun.
The sun is shining,
shining bright,
as the waves roll in.

The children's laugh,
has now died out.
The beach is empty,
once again.
The silent watchers,
now dark in shadow,
still look on,
as the waves roll in.

The day is done,
the people have left.
The sun burns out,

and quickly sinks.
The night arrives,
with all its splendor,
as the waves roll in.

Jeff Wiesen
Age: 13

DUCKS

In Star Park lives a duck named Bobby,
Who sometimes can be very naughty.
He likes to eat bread
Whenever he's fed
With his best friend whose name is Glotty.

Lisa Bassi
Age: 11

PEOPLE

People,
Different sizes, different shapes, brown,
White, tan, freckles,
People

Matt Bernstein
Age: 10

WITCHES

When I see a witch it freaks me out,
eek
I see one
it looks like my sister
aaaaaaaaaaaahhh!
I live with one.

Ashley Christensen
Age: 10

MY, UH... WALLS

My walls, map of my consciousness,
drawings, writings, and colorful
designs sprout on the 106
year old, brown walls.

A marker yells in pain,
as my clumsy friend steps on it
causing a horrible pain
forcing silver blood out of the marker
oozing on the floor.

My walls,
home of different feelings
expressed.

Harley Burkhart
Age: 13

SKELETON WORLD

They come from a land from a faraway place
thcy cat whatever they see.

So you don't want to go in a graveyard tonight...
you might be seen.

Don't worry... you will be one soon.

BOO!!

Jason Fong
Age: 10

JANE HADLEY KWETT

Jane
Friendly, nice, smart
Sister of Allyson and Michael
Lover of my family, reading, Ginger
Who feels strongly about recycling
Soccer, relay races
Hadley
Who needs food shelter friends
Who gives advice, toys, clothes
Who fears heights, bombs, bad grades
Would like to see Europe
A resident of San Rafael, California.
Kwett

Jane Kwett
Age: 9

HALLOWEEN

Halloween is a time for trick or treating.
Halloween is a time for eating candy.
Halloween is a time for staying up late.
Halloween is a time for having fun.

Elizabeth Harris
Age: 9

EASTER

Easter is in the month of April.
There are eggs, Easter hunts,
candy, and lots of other things.
When Easter is here,
children are happy and they have lots of fun.

Liza Castaneda
Age: 9

My dog is black and white with a pink collar.
My dog likes to chase her tail.
My dog looks very funny when she does that.
My dog can really sail.
My dog is very funny that way because
She chases her tail.
My dog's name is Polka.
My dog is very funny that way.

Carli Kaufman
Age: 9

FANTASY

Fantasies are so much fun,
I love to dream them one by one.
Some are fun, some are not.
Some are sad, some are bad.
Just hope you dream at least ONE!

Dwila Hyppolite
Age: 11

California
A wesome
L ong
I ndians
F ood
O ranges
R eptiles
N atives
I nteresting
A wkward

Elizabeth Teasdale

TEARS

As a teardrop falls from eye to cheek
I know what disappointment is.
Upon a cloud I wish to be
Floating away in the gentle breeze
Softly, softly I float away
Without a care in the world
More tears are left to come
Hiding away behind my eyes.
Oh how I wish to be on a cloud
Instead of a lonely room without a drop of love
Ten tears for a drop of love would be
A simple price to pay
If only a drop of love would take my tears away.

Amyleigh Casselman
Age: 9

THE BLUEBIRD

I once saw a bluebird fly,
Its wings beat bright,
Against the pale blue of the sky.

As I watched that bluebird fly,
I knew with a queer dull pain,
That nothing would seem so blue to me again.

Timmy Tirrell
Age: 9

THE FLOWERING

It has begun....
Vale, mountain, meadow
I stand upon the mountain top.
Part my lips then here an echo
I lay across the meadow
Flowers shining upon my footstep.
Ocean, lake, river
I stay afloat the lake
Seeing it glistening
Riding the waves
Upon it's wavering flow.
The spell is broken
NEVERMORE

Helen Chang
Age: 13

GREEN

A sea of green everywhere,
A never ending stream,
A non-ceasing ocean,
Like a beautiful dream
I see this color everywhere I go,
Sometimes waving to and fro,
Sometimes still.

Luke Pollock
Age: 9

NATASHA ALEXANDRIA KAWAHARA

Natasha
Helpful, nice and sweet.
Sister of Christopher
Lover of bike riding, skating and music.
Who feels strongly about health,
Friendship and the environment.
Alexandria
Who needs skates, a bike and a family
Who gives gifts, cards and books.
Who fears spiders, bees and bears.
Would like to see Japan.
A resident of San Rafael, California.
Kawahara

Natasha Kawahara
Age: 9

THE CHRISTMAS TREE

No one is hanging stockings up.
No one is baking pie.
No one is talking brotherhood.
No one is looking up to see a new star in the sky.
No one loves a Christmas tree on the 24th of July.

Teairah Wilson
Age: 11

CARS

Cars are red,
motorcycles are blue,
I love Deloreans
and so do you!!!
I think?

Andrew Stewart
Age: 10

LIFE AND DEATH

We all know that we're going to die someday.
It's so hard to go away.
But we're all going to die someday.
Have fun with life and when you're ready
To die, let out your heart and cry.
Some people die a peaceful death,
And some die a violent death.
But just remember all the things in
Life and you will be a part of it.
Life is good, but death will come, someday.

Elizabeth Forsland
Age: 8

TRISHA

T errific
R ooster *
I ntelligent
S neaky
H appy
A +

All these things describe
the way I am.
It's ME!

*Chinese Zodiac animal year

Trisha Quan
Age: 12

AFTER DARK

After the sun sets it slowly gets dark.
The sky turns colors, yellow, blue,
purple, red, pink, orange, and white.
The sunsets are beautiful.
I like them a lot.
After dark the crickets start
to make noises like a violin.
The children that play, slowly
go to their snug homes.
Their parents read a story of the
beautiful fairies that sparkle
and shimmer in the moonlight.
When everyone is in their beds all
snug and warm the wind outside
blows so hard it makes the house
feel like it is going to fly
right off into the dark sky.
At night if or when a storm rises
the rain pores like cats and dogs.
It makes puddles the size of ponds.
I love the night so beautiful and mysterious.

Kelly Smith
Age: 12

IF I COULD TRAVEL THROUGH TIME

If I could travel through time,
Just think of what fun it would be!
I could go to any time and anywhere.
Imagine all the things I could see!

I could go back six million years,
When all the dinosaurs were on the go.
I'll try not to land under a dinosaur's foot,
For fear that I would be crushed like snow.

Or I could travel to the future,
To see what would become of me.
Will I become a millionaire,
Or will I be as poor as can be?

Will cars travel faster than sound?
Will cars be hooked on laser tracks?
Will cars be controlled by computers?
Will cars park in electronic racks?

If I could travel through time,
I won't have many more questions to ask.
Because the answers to all my questions,
Would be such an easy task!

Charles Yong
Age: 8

MY FRIEND STEPHANIE

Stephanie's hair is black coal.
Her skin is a brown dried leaf.
She is as neat as neat can be.
She can hold a box with 14 bottles.
Her voice is a violin.
Her ideas are creative.
She is a growing tree.
Her skin is smooth plastic.
And that's my friend Steph.

Michelle Levin
Age: 7

CHRISTMAS

Christmas Christmas
Oh how I like it!
Christmas is in December
Christmas is fun.
It's with your family
It's with your friends
You'll open presents
You'll be surprised.
Get a Christmas tree
Decorate it too!
Sing Christmas carols
I can hardly wait
Can You?

Julianne Donohoe
Age: 8

GO AWAY SUN

Sunny go away
You're burning my eyes.
Come back another sunrise.
Go away sun.
How you shine
I brought my shades
At the five and dime.

Jonathan Richardson
Age: 8

The summer is over
The leaves are falling
Winter is on it's way
The birds are calling
For snow to start falling
Someday someday
Someday...
The drought is over
The streams are filling and flowing
The flowers
Are freezing and glowing
The summer's over the
Winter is here
Summer's over
Spring is soon near

Casey Newman
Age: 11

LITTLE BOY ON THE MOON

Little boy on the moon
here I call so faraway
It is doubtful that you can hear me
but this is what I say

Little boy on the moon
is it scary so high in the sky
Little boy on the moon
where do you hide at day

Do you hide by the White Dwarf star
or by the Milky Way
Let me know little boy dear
because to me you look so near

Holly Beth Stimson
Age: 10

RAIN

I love it when it rains
I also love the sound
I like to splash in puddles
And get really wet
I like to sip apple cider
On rainy days.

Lauren Baxter
Age: 9

AN OCTOBER EVENING SKY

An October evening sky
the sunlight reflected
on the moon,
the stars
twinkling bright
the earth turning slowly
I stood still
on my deck
thinking how
they blend together.

Jon Venezia
Age: 8

EIGHT

Eight, eight it's just great!
You can ride a bike, hike or even skate.
Being eight is better than five
You are almost old enough to drive
I can't think of anything better
Except maybe a brand new sweater
When will I be nine?
Oh well, I have plenty of time
For now eight is fine with me
Perhaps tomorrow I will climb a tree.

Susan J. Schultz
Age: 8

WHAT'S GOING ON, HELP!

Only one can see through the eyes of itself.
Pictures appear in front of you,
wild flowing colors gasping your breath
out of your mouth,
figures of people roam in front of you,
you can see the light through the pupil of your eye,
the biggest trip you have ever been on
is right in front of you
everything in front of you wouldn't be there
if it wasn't for the eye, back and forth,
open and shut it's all the same
to the one who can see, but wait,
you've awakened from a dark sleep
trying to open your eyes but you can't
everything's dark and scary,
you're struggling to see,
fighting the pain
digging your cold sweaty hands
into your eyes and face,
hoping you can rub this death threat away,
but yet you can't, it's there,
still struggling your eyes just won't open,
you feel as if you're dead,
but actually you are in some way,
because you've been robbed of something
so magnificent
your sight,
you are blind.
How are you going to live, survive...you won't?

                                        Jennifer McDonough

RYAN PAUL CINKO

Ryan
Nice, kind, and funny
Brother of Andreas
Lover of reading, family and basketball
Who feels strongly about recycling,
Ozone layer and animals
Paul
Who needs money, a college education, and a Sega
Who gives my work, my pencils and pens
Who fears spiders, snakes and rats
Would like to see Brazil
A resident of Novato, California
Cinko

Ryan Gibney Cinko
Age: 9

DIFFERENT PEOPLE

There are all different kinds of people, there are:
Fat, skinny, short, tall, fast, and stubby people
but there are also different colors of people,
there are blue, purple, brown, green, yellow, orange,
and red, but it doesn't matter if you're
fat, skinny, short, tall, fast, or stubby
or what color you are what matters is what's inside.

Allie Boyer

THE QUEEN OF MY DREAMS

There is a woman in a long white gown,
Who I often see in my sleep.
A woman in a long white gown,
She's there though she never makes a peep.

Her face is pale and plain,
Her eyes like dewdrops of rain.
Her smile is small,
Yet kind and bright as the sun.
But her frown is like a thunderstorm of rage and hate.

When she is sad she cries,
And when she cries, it's like soft rain coming
From the pale blue sky.

She has an imagination like none other.
She is the queen of my dreams.

Mariam Missaghi
Age: 10

FISH

Fish are slimy, neat, and fast.
They live in oceans, rivers, or lakes.
Fish eat smaller fish, worms, fish eggs.
People have them for pets.
They swim in schools with other fish.

Jimmy Hart
Age: 10

LIFE

The roots grow,
  getting stronger
  and stretching
   to the sky.

  The bud
  young and helpless,
    getting bigger
   day by day.

As it reaches its highest growing point,
   It opens,
    expanding
  by the light of the sun,
   and the freshness
    of the water
      on its roots.

  The petals separate from
    each other
     as the air
    reaches the pollen
      for the first time.

   But soon
  the delicate petals
    start to whither away, die,
      and fall off the stem,

   Which they

```
                had once
          hung onto
                for dear life.
```

Sara Kamins
Age: 13

WHO AM I?

I am not the girl who lives down the street.
I am not the ballerina with pointed feet.
I am not a detective in disguise.
I am not an elephant, big in size.

I am not a teacher, strict and mean.
I am not a twig, fragile and lean.
I am not a crying baby, hard to soothe.
I am not a silky fabric, soft and smooth.

I am not the gymnast on a balance beam.
I am not a scientist with a crazy scheme.
I am not an angel in a cloud.
I am not a trumpet, big and loud.

I am myself in my own way,
And that is how I'll always stay.
Never forget I'll always be me,
Because that is all I want to be.

Celina Yong
Age: 14

APPRECIATION

Appreciate what
You have

Appreciate the people
Around you

Love them,
Cherish them,

Hold tight to things
Dear to you

Most of all,
To the people dear to you

Maybe, if you
Hold them close
To your heart

They will still be
There tomorrow

And if they are not
You will know you

Have made the best
Of what you had

Jodie Konigsberg
Age: 13

THANKSGIVING

People always have a big, big feast.
People have families.
They have pies and turkey.
People always have THANKSGIVING!

Sarah Bradford
Age: 9

CHRISTMAS

Christmas! Christmas!
Oh, how I like Christmas.
Holly hung upon the wall
Lots of happiness short and tall.
Carols being sung
By the Christmas tree all aglow.
Stockings by the fireplace
Waiting to be filled.
Christmas! Christmas!
Oh, how I like Christmas.
It fills my mind with pride and joy
To think of Christmas.
But what makes Christmas so special?
Could it be that it comes but once a year?
I bet you can guess
This is my favorite time of year.
Christmas! Christmas!
Oh, how I like Christmas.

Sarah J. Wintermeyer
Age: 8

CHRISTMAS

C an you
H old the
R ing and put
I t on the angel?
S o can you put
T he ring on the angel?
M erry Christmas!
A nd
S ave up to buy Christmas presents!

Nathaniel D'Angelo
Age: 9

THE RIVER

The river runs,
The water flows,
The people come,
The people go,
Everywhere things are coming and going,
Everywhere life is flowing,
If life should stop,
Then I will drop,
If life should go,
Then I will flow,
Like the river.

Stuart Taines

PIES, PIES, YUMMY, YUMMY PIES!

Strawberry, raspberry, blackberry, blueberry pies.
They're so delicious!
Delicious I say -
Makes me want to eat pies till I die!

Michael Mendoza
Age: 9

LITTLE INDIAN

There is an Indian in the moonlight and-
He hunts for his dinner.
In the sunlight he fetches water.
In the dreary, dark night he sleeps.
Sleep little Indian for the time will pass fast.

Nicole Gallagher
Age: 9

OCTOBER EVENING SKIES

Underneath the fallen skies
The moon out my window
I see the moon
The moon the moon I fall asleep
Underneath the moon.

Matthew Huntsman
Age: 9

THE NIGHT SKY

The night sky is black
The stars are bright
The moon man is out tonight
The moon is shining across the seas
Here I come it's me! See!

Antone Haley
Age: 8

LITTLE BOYS AND GIRLS OF SPACE

Little boy Thrindle
here I come with a little bit of earth,

Little boy Milky Way is shy
he wishes to be human,

Little girl Ember
she wants a little dog
she does not want to be seen,

Little girl Star up in the sky
shining so bright
I admire from the start,

Little boys and girls
I love you all
and you and me will keep it a secret.

Kimy Ventresca
Age: 8

THE MAN IN THE MOON

There was a man who lived in the moon
He was moved by the sun around the earth
He saw the stars above the sky
And when he saw them he began to cry

Rebecca Spaletta
Age: 8

BLACK

Black is an oven
And black is a street
And black is the wrapper
On my candy bar treat.

Black are the walls
And black is the floor
And black is the paint
On my aunt's door.

And now my poem
Has come to an end
So let black be
Your best color, friend.

Geoffrey Bass
Age: 9

THE THINGS IN SPACE

I like the stars.
I like the planets
But most of all
I like the asteroids,
The asteroid is large and cruel
It destroys everything in its path.

Jasen Robinson
Age: 9

GREEN

Green is the color
Of the leaves on trees,
Also pickles, olives and peppers.
Mint ice cream
(Which I like the best.)
And a one dollar bill
To spend on it
Mouthwash and a 7-Up can
Plus a green salad with dinner
Finally,
    the stem
        on a
           tomato.

Marie Newsom
Age: 9

THE STAR DIPPER

Every night
I watch the star dipper.
Every night
at 8:00 o'clock
I see the beautiful shine
of the stars that make
the star named
The Big Dipper.

Kate Kiechle
Age: 10

MY CAT TIE-DYE

My cat Tie-Dye is a mountain climber
That never stops climbing.
She is a leopard that runs like a bullet;
A giant that drinks all of the milk in the world.
She's furry as a dog that never stops growing fur.
She's as soft as a rabbit.
She acts like she is always tired.
Her nails are as sharp as a razor.
Her fur is a million colors.
She is as big as a log.
Tie-Dye is my cat.

Spencer W. Drotman
Age: 7

MY RAT, MITZI

My rat is as strong as the wind.
My rat is as soft as cotton.
My rat is as sweet as chocolate.
My rat is a dolphin.
That's my rat.

Tay Feder
Age: 7

THE SUN AND THE MOON

In the night
the moon shines bright
a star shines bright
up high
but excuse me
where is the sun?

Molly Livingston
Age: 9

SQUEEKEE

She is as light as a feather.
She is as white as snow.
She is a small eraser.
She is the wind.
She has eyes like rubies.
She has a tail as long as a ruler.
She has cotton fur.
Her nose is as pink as bubble gum.
She is a sweet marshmallow.
She is as cuddly as a kitten.
She's a playful puppy.
She is a mouse that never stops squeaking.
She eats like a pig.
That's my mouse Squeekee.

Tanisha LaBelle
Age: 7

MY RAT COOKIE

She is as soft as a bunny.
She is a clown.
She is a hibernating bear at sleep.
She's as small as a name card.
She has bear's claws.
A road runner is as fast.
She is a cookie when she sleeps.
A Dalmatian has spots like Cookie.
Her eyes are like chocolate chips.
She is as fragile as a glass doll.
I love her and she loves me.
That's my Cookie.

Sadie Walker
Age: 7

TO A BEST FRIEND

I promise to stay through the rain
And I told you I'd stick close through the pain.
I promise to go the extra mile,
And when you're feeling down
Will volunteer the smile.
'Cause you're my best friend
And I'm there
Just say when
And I will love ya 'til the end.
Even though they'll be tough times
We won't agree
But the love we share will always be.
I will tell you
When right and when wrong
'Cause it's the truth I love
And always take along.
This friendship I treasure
God gave is mine
He made us best friends
And I will love ya
'Till the end.

Courtney C. Chan
Age: 15

SADNESS

Sadness is like a warm bright summer day
Being covered with thick heavy smoke and tears.
Sadness is someone being taken from you.
It could feel like they are gone years or only seconds.
Sadness is like a bright red rose.
Its smell taunts you, but
When you come close, it pricks you.
You and your heart.
Sadness is misery, horrible, dark and gloomy.
Misery is like you are in a different world.
You're not aware of anything.
Sadness is gloom, like oceans of tears
Come into your body
And a knife stabs you in the heart
And oceans of tears start streaming out.

Stephanie Sidjakov
Age: 11

ROBERT CHARLES HAMER

Robert
Brother of Kyle, Dillon, Chris and Marissa
Lover of family, friends and reading
Who feels strongly about painting,
Keeping people happy and freedom.
Charles
Who needs family, food, shelter
Who gives candy, presents, and shelter
Who fears snakes, spiders.
Would like to see the Mona Lisa
A resident of San Rafael and Mill Valley, California
Hamer

Robert C. Hamer IV
Age: 9

THE ANIMAL

An animal without fur nor hair,
You can see it soaring through the air,
It can run, it can swim it can fly,
But this animal is really quite shy,
It paddles with its small webbed feet,
Through the water, for something to eat,
It has feathers and a beak,
During winter, South it will seek,
When in danger it escapes with luck,
This graceful animal is a duck.

Gavin Howell
Age: 13

CRAZY DREAM

I wrote this poem to say,
or should I put it this way....
I had a dream and,
I wasn't so clean
I went to the store and,
fell upon the floor
So I took a shower that
came out flour
Then I went out for toast,
looking like a ghost
Before I got to the next block,
a woman came out with a shock and,
she gave me a knock
So I ran into a shop but,
before long,
it didn't seem,
to be a dream.

Yer Cheng

GRANDMA

I am here to tell you
About a little old lady named Sue.
She is my granny,
She sits on her fanny,
And sings a song called Loo,
Loo, loo, loo MOO.
She sings it day and night.
'Turn on the light'
She says to me,
'And we will feel free, so free.'
Early in the morn,
She gets an awful scorn,
As she sprays the potpourri.
For dinner each night, when she feeds me,
It's liver and beans,
And sauerkraut cheese.
She says it is healthy,
It makes her get wealthy.
But she lives in a shack,
Right by the seas.
Her kisses are slimy,
Her voice is all whiny.
And that my friend is why,
Your going to fly,
To see my dear granny.

Kathryn Blaisdell
Age: 11

BEAUTIFUL GIRL

I know a beautiful girl,
Ever since the first day of school
I would look at her, and my heart would drool
With her hair so fair, her face so square
If I could, I would hug and kiss her;
And when I'm alone, I'd be on drugs and
miss her
Her face, unforgettable,
Her expression, inextinguishable
And if I could give her everything, I would.

I know a beautiful girl,
She talks, so sweetly
She walks, so neatly
Her face, so full of grace--
That when she stands by my side,
I'd wish she was my bride
To her, I give my full attention
And if she hates me, when I get suspension,
I'd still love her, with my whole devotion.

If she feels sorrow, I'd feel pain
And if she wants me tomorrow, I'll be happy
again.

I know a beautiful girl,
That I await, and wish that she'd come, and be
my mate
But if she gets blindness, from my kindness
Then I'd help her see through, and look at
The real me, that'll be renew.

Yes this girl, is so pretty, that she is
meant, For the whole world to see--
And wonder about, her luscious beauty.

Thavisack Syphanthong
Age: 14

SUNSETS

The sun sets across the sky,
Filling the world with wonder and pride,
People seek across the land,
Woman and child, man and man.
Sunsets are the most beautiful things,
Birds fly across sunsets with two powerful wings.

Katie Haberman

CARS

Cars are big.
Cars are small.
Cars are colorful.
Cars are cool.
Cars arc bad.
I like cars.

Chris Garabedian
Age: 11

WRITE

A book can take you to the
    SKY,
Authors have found a new way to
    FLY,
   You could be one if you
    TRY,
There isn't any trick, you have
    nothing to
    BUY,
This is the truth and I will never
    LIE,
Just take a pen, and you can soar
    HIGH!!!!

Kristina Walker
Age: 11

THE LIGHTNING IN ARIZONA

When I lived in Arizona,
I loved it when it stormed,
Why, you ask,
Because I like the way it looks.
The way it sounds.
The lightning in Arizona is a
lot more beautiful than here.
Here!
In Arcata, of course.
It's yellow and pink and white.
The lightning in Arizona.

Christy Edwards
Age: 11

STINKY, SLIMY REPTILES

Stinky, slimy reptiles are the things
that I hate most.
They slither and they slime
around the crumbly old fence posts.

They blink their eyes,
their tongues hang out,
then little girls
begin to shout.

Their tails fall off
on the ground,
You find their skin
lying around.

They climb up your legs
and on your arms,
but people say they
do no harm.

Humans like to have
them for pets,
But as for me,
I like them dead.

Sarah Warvi
Age: 11

THE LADY WHO LIVED BY THE SEA

There once was an old lady
who lived by the sea.
Her name was Matilda,
Matilda McGee.
She wanted a monkey,
A monkey, you see.
But she thought a monkey
shouldn't live by the sea.
So she moved to the city
and wanted a kitty.
But the city is no place
for a kitty.
So she moved to Moscow
And wanted a cow.
But Moscow is no place
for a cow.
So she packed up her bags
and moved to the same old
place by the sea.
There she'll stay,
Matilda, Matilda,
Matilda McGee,
The lady who lived by the sea.

Radenna Foreman
Age: 12

PESKY SISTER

You think she would be as sweet as spice,
but she really isn't nice!

She's pesky and messy and gets into your stuff,
you wish she didn't do anything!
But of course you have that pesky sister in your stuff.

Sisters are messy, pesky, and hit you, too!
They really aren't sweet,
but everyone thinks they are, too!

What is it with those people?
Are they under some kinda spell?

She gets what she wants,
She gets ME in trouble
What is it with these people?
She is never in trouble!

You wish you were an only child,
the one to be loved,
but you have that pesky sister that gets into your stuff!

Well I guess she isn't that bad,
'Oh great, I better go,
that pesky sister is in my stuff!

April Ledesma
Age: 11

BORN IN A SHOE

I couldn't believe it,
I was born in a shoe,
My mom said she was, too.
My parents, my grandparents,
they were born in a cup,
So I guess the shoe
was my rotten luck.
I don't have a normal life,
I go swimming in mud puddles
on hot summer days,
I swing on shoe laces
all different ways.
Guess where my room is?
It's in the toe,
I have to slide down
and lay low.
My biggest fear is that
someone might come along,
Put my shoe on
and be on their way.

Ramanda Smith
Age: 11

THE WOODS

Deep in the dark woods where the coyotes howl
Deep in the dark woods where the werewolves
prowl
Deep in the dark woods late at night,
where your only friend is the pale moonlight.

Deep in the dark woods nature's playground
Deep in the dark woods I think I'll lay down
Deep in the dark woods on the cold ground,
As I sleep the werewolves start to surround.

Deep in the dark woods where I lay
Deep in the dark woods I'll fight all day
Deep in the dark woods in the stench of decay,
I'll fight the werewolves and make them pay.

So never go in the dark woods late at night
Where your only friend is the pale moonlight
Where you fight the werewolves with all your might,
For I found out the hard way.

Billy Stonebarger
Age: 11

MY SHEEP

I have some stupid sheep.
But I love my stupid sheep.
One day my sheep.
Wrecked in a jeep.
The awe fell in a heap in the jeep.
I was deep in sorrow.
I thought my stupid sheep were dead.
Then my sheep beeped
The horn in a heap in a jeep
They will leap to me
Then I will keep my stupid sheep
In a heap in the jeep.

Amber Jade Gibbens
Age: 10

STREAMS

Streams to me are like smooth,
cool bumpy ice.

As cool as the evening breeze,

As smooth as polished gold.

Surrounded by tall quiet trees,
it runs as swiftly as the wind.

Every time I see it, I feel like a white feather
running through the trees.

Nolan Civian
Age: 10

BIKES

I like bikes
When I was little
I had a trike.
Then I was too big
For a trike.
So I got a bike
with training wheels.
One day I didn't need
training wheels.
Then I got a bike
that had no training wheels.
The bike was the best bike
in the world.

Paul Hailey
Age: 10

THE BOOGIE MAN

I woke up once in the night,
thought about the boogie man,
it game me a fright.
You better watch out, he's coming
after you. At any time he could
come out of the blue.

Joey Vance
Age: 12

HIDDEN PICTURES

I see eight different animals in this picture
or more.
You don't see these animals every time you
walk out of doors.
These animals are endangered,
so let them roam around.
Animals belong to the wild.
Watch their beauty as they walk,
fly or soar.
From mountain to mountain
sea to tree,
please let these animals
roam and be free.
The mountains trees and seas
are their homes.
The clouds are where the
birds play and roam.
The glittering snow on the mountain tops,
this picture reminds me of home.

Barbara Ann Hudson
Age: 11

FIRE

Blazing bright
All colors red, yellow, clear and blue
Ouch, better not touch it or you will get burned.

Corey Leavitt

WHY DO THEY LEAVE US SO SOON?

Why, oh Lord, is life so cruel?
So unfair, confusing, and unkind?
Why can't we live forever?
And change our thought of mind?

Why do you take away our loved ones?
And leave us here alone?
To mourn and suffer in this unfair world,
With our hearts as cold as stone.

Why is mankind so strange and unwise?
And why is our life so short?
Why do we become so attached to each other,
And cry until our eyes hurt?

Why do people die so soon,
Right when their life is so good?
Why can't they live a bit longer?
I'm sure they would if they could.

Allison Largent
Age: 12

The wind is as cold as ice.
The water is as blue as the sky.
The sand is as soft as cotton.
The water is as salty as salt.
That's what makes the sea special!

Maria Rubalcava
Age: 10

175

I WILL ALWAYS REMEMBER THAT DAY

I will always remember that day;
it was Martin Luther King's birthday.
This time I had to say good-bye
and I hope my cat, Sam, will try
to remember her past
for she lived long and that day was her last.
We had to put my cat to sleep.
I didn't want to watch her go into that
deep sleep
for I knew she wouldn't make a peep.

Although I am only eleven
and my sister is two years older than seven,
I hope my cat, Sam, has a good time in heaven.

She is finally 'free at last'
and I hope she will remember her past.

Nicole Braafladt
Age: 11

THE TREE

There was a tree taller than me
Until I cut it down
Then it was smaller -
Than me!

Russell Stewart
Age: 9

MY THOUGHTS

Sometimes, somedays, my thoughts are as the
   rain-cold, dark, and crying.
Sometimes, some days, my thoughts are as the
   sun-glistening, shining and happy.
Sometimes, some days, my feelings are as a lion
   cub-restlessly unable to sleep because of troubles.
Sometimes, some days, my feelings are as a
   pet-faithful and happy in his place.
Sometimes, some days, I feel just like dirt-
   unwanted, down trodden.
Sometimes, some days I feel just like a
   rainbow-loved, like someone cares.
Sometimes, some days, my thoughts and
   feelings make me wish I were gone.
Sometimes, some days, my thoughts and
   feelings make me happier than ever, it seems.
But I know, however I feel, there's always
   someone somewhere who cares, even if we're apart.

Julie A. Burbridge

CHRISTMAS

Christmastime is here to stay.
Angels fly and love to play.
When happy tears and trees go away -
That means Christmas has gone away!

Casey Cassano
Age: 10

MY DREAMS

Some days my dreams are like
  kittens - soft gentle and loving.
Some days my dreams are like
  rollercoasters - exciting and thrilling.
Some days my dreams are like
  a puppy looking through a store window - sad.
Some days my dreams are like
  teddy bears - something to hold on to.
Some days my dreams are like
  butterflies - soft, beautiful, and elegant.
Some days my dreams are like
  flowers - some beautiful and some ugly.
Some days my dreams are like
  leaves - all different.
Some days my dreams are like
  rainbows - colorful a making people wish.
But all the same they're mine, and no one else's

Nicole E. Anderson
Age: 11

BLUEBIRD

Blue bird flapping its wings against the storm lit sky,
Hovering over the ground looking for some food,
Having the wind beat against its purple, blue wings
And BANG it falls into the rustling leaves.

Laird Norgeot

OCEAN

I like the ocean
you like the ocean.
I like the color
of the water
all over the
world.

Annie Huynh
Age: 10

The mountains were tall and proud,
around my face they sang aloud.
A beautiful tune that carried my soul
around the coast above and below.

Mia Sakai

IN THIS LIFE

This cup is overflowing;
Fertile like a mother.
Natural earthy tones
Like a watercolor,
Washed in deep hues:
Amber in autumn,
Ashen white in winter,
Green during spring,
Flaxen in the summer.

Wilderness hides abounding life:
Mushrooms thrusting upward,
Concealed in the loam.
A doe camouflaged in the foliage;
Leaping out with a bound,
Melting again into pines.
Running down a forest path,
Branches rake their fingers
Through my tangled hair.
A raven watches me from a limb
Of an ancient redwood who's seen
Many seasons come and go,
Animals born and gone,
And the earth deteriorates as
Humans throw caution to the wind.

The sun is a face in the sky.
I wish I were positive
That it is smiling down at me.
The wind carries a chill;

Grim fog cloaks the halo.
A warning of what is to come
In this life.

Heather Flynn
Age: 14

My poems have been fun to share
Through the California air.

Rachel Rubin
Age: 7

I see a rabbit
he is hopping in the field
looking for his prey.

Alan Christopher Lee
Age: 11

My talent
active, fun
bursting, moving, alive
anywhere, anytime, neat, special
a real live verb

Allyson Criner
Age: 9

There once was a Thanksgiving with bread and rice.
We had a feast with some great mice.
I ate 6 turkeys I became nice.
Since I was so fat from eating
I was the turkey instead.

Scott Ngai
Age: 8

MY DAD

My dad is an energizer.
He is stronger than steel.
He is a million bucks.
My dad is a window that never will be broken.
My dad is the sun.
He runs around with me.
I learn what's right and wrong.
He is a muscle man with glasses.

Sean T. McNeil
Age: 7

MY FRIEND SCOTT

Scott is as big as two trees together.
He is as skinny as a ruler.
His skin is as soft as a pillow.
He is Superman.
He is as fast as a cheetah.
He is a tiger.
He acts like a monkey.
He's silly and I like Scott.

Jake Lipton
Age: 7

FALL LEAVES

Down, down
Yellow and brown.
The leaves are falling
All over the ground.

Down, down
Orange and red.
The leaves are
Like a soft bed.

Suzy Goad
Age: 11

MY SQUEAKY

My Squeaky is as small as a beetle.
Her fur is as smooth as silk.
She has fur as gold as golden corn.
She has eyes like diamond rubies.
As pretty as a gold rabbit.
She is as fluffy as a pillow.
She is as hungry as a bear.
My Squeaky is a mouse.

Mara Mayock
Age: 7

My dogs are faster than a cheetah.
Lassie and Penny are more colorful than a rainbow.
My dogs are sneakier than the tooth fairy.
My pets eat more that 250 ants.
They are my best friends.

Cameron Waldman
Age: 7

MY DAD

My dad is a gold nugget in a mine.
He is a loving dad.
He is the sun and I am the moon.
We will always be together.
I love my dad.
He is a whale.
When I hug him, he feels hairy.
I know that he loves me.
I trust him.
That's my dad.

Courtney Piper
Age: 7

MY FRIEND JAMES

My friend James is as nice as a bird.
He's as funny as a joke.
He is a $100,000.
He is going home.
'Bye, bye', says James.
James makes up weird songs.
He is the tallest kid in the world.
This is James for you.

Jonathan Reali
Age: 7

My cat is as strong as a lion.
He is as wild as a tiger.
He is bad like a rattlesnake.
My cat bites like a cobra.
He is a pencil attacker.
He is slime sometimes.
He's weird with his ears back,
Like my brother.
That's my cat, Elvis.

Gregory Lynch
Age: 7

DAN MY MAN

My friend Danny is as cool as a glacier
that never cracks.
He is as intelligent as an eagle.
He is an Orca.
My friend Danny is a corner kick in the goal.
He is up to my mouth in height.
He sounds like an Orca singing underwater.
My friend is just so, so, so cool.
That's my man, Dan.

Matt Silver
Age: 7

FEAST OF THANKSGIVING

I see the turkey golden brown.
I see the moonlight showing like a crown.
I see the bronze showing on the leaves.
I see the gold jumping in the breeze.
I see Thanksgiving coming in the air.
I see Thanksgiving everywhere!

Lulu Waks
Age: 9

THANKSGIVING FEAST

Thank you Earth for the Indians and Pilgrims
That made up the first Thanksgiving feast

Thank you for the turkey, potatoes,
And dressing that we eat!

Thank you for the
THANKSGIVING FEAST!

THANK YOU!

Daisy Lowery
Age: 10